Essential Golden Retriever Quick Reference Card

Your Dog's Name ____________________

Name on Your Dog's Pedigree (if applicable) ____________________

Where Your Dog Was Purchased ____________________

Address ____________________

Phone Number ____________________

Your Dog's Birthday ____________________

Your Dog's Veterinarian ____________________

Address ____________________

Phone Number ____________________

Emergency Number ____________________

Your Dog's Health

Vaccines

Type ____________________ *Date Given* ___/___/___

Type ____________________ *Date Given* ___/___/___

Type ____________________ *Date Given* ___/___/___

Type ____________________ *Date Given* ___/___/___

Heartworm

Date Tested ___/___/___ *Type Used* ____________________ *Start Date* ___/___/___

Your Dog's License Number ____________________

Groomer's Name and Phone Number ____________________

Dog Sitter/Walker's Name and Phone Number ____________________

External Features of a Golden Retriever

THE

ESSENTIAL

Golden Retriever

Consulting Editor

IAN DUNBAR, PH.D., MRCVS

Featuring Photographs by

RENÉE STOCKDALE

HOWELL
BOOK
HOUSE

Howell Book House
A Simon & Schuster Macmillan Company
1633 Broadway
New York, NY 10019

Macmillan Publishing books may be purchased for business or sales promotional use. For information please write: Special Markets Department, Macmillan Publishing USA, 1633 Broadway, New York, NY 10019.

The Essential Golden Retriever is an abridged edition of *The Golden Retriever: An Owner's Guide to a Happy Healthy Pet,* first published in 1995.

Library of Congress Cataloging-in-Publication Data
The essential golden retriever/featuring photographs by Renée Stockdale
p. cm.
Includes bibliographical references and index.
1. Golden Retriever I. Howell Book House.
SF429.g63E77 1998 98-3415
636.752'7—dc21 CIP

ISBN 0-87605-345-2

Manufactured in the United States of America
10 9 8 7 6 5 4 3 2 1

Series Directors: Dominique DeVito, Donald Stevens
Series Assistant Directors: Jennifer Liberts, Amanda Pisani
Editorial Assistant: Michele Matrisciani
Photography Editor: Sarah Storey
Production Team: Stephanie Mohler, Heather Pope, Karen Teo
Book Design: Paul Costello
Cover Photography: Renée Stockdale

Many Golden Retrievers in interior photos courtesy of Cedarwood Kennels and Jan Grant. Photos pages 76, 80 and 81 courtesy of Diana Robinson.

Contents

CHAPTER ONE

Getting to Know Your Golden Retriever

Most of us seek our first Golden Retriever because we are attracted to his physical appearance, reputation as a family dog and overall good temperament. The majority of Goldens live up to these expectations and usually exceed them. The behavior traits described in this chapter are the reactions of a typical Golden Retriever.

Unlike some breeds, which tend to be one-person or single-family oriented, a Golden shares his affections freely with many. He will form an especially strong bond with the person who might be his primary trainer or whoever spends the most time with him, but never to the exclusion of others. This trait, along with a Golden's overt friendliness, is a deterrent to someone seeking a dog that is protective or wary of strangers. Typically, Goldens do not make good

Characteristics of the Golden Retriever

Loves people
Very trustworthy
Easily adapts to new situations
Highly trainable
Eager retriever, happy to carry things around
Friendly, outgoing and exuberant

guard dogs. They are generally not excessive barkers, though they will alert their owners to unusual incidents such as strange sounds or intruders. While dogs of other breeds might bark, growl and even threaten a stranger, a Golden is most likely to bark and wag his tail in greeting.

Golden Retrievers are renowned for their friendly, trustworthy and affectionate natures.

Goldens naturally seem to trust humans. This is why they are among the favorite clients of veterinarians, dog groomers and obedience instructors. Along with trust is the inherent ability to forgive. Many owners could learn from their Goldens. A Golden will take a normal correction, given fairly, in stride. He will learn from it and continue to like and respect the person who administered it. A traumatic incident will not affect a Golden for any length of time. He will go on with life, tail wagging.

It is this resiliency and an ability to adapt to new situations that makes the Golden ideal for so many different purposes. Dogs used in guiding the blind, assisting the deaf, providing therapy to old or infirm people must be able to enter any situation or environment and continue to put the tasks of the job ahead of any other distractions.

Goldens crave affection and will demand it. As a whole, male members of the breed tend to be more attentive and affectionate than females, who are often more independent in nature. They will want to be petted, and some will even stick their noses under an arm and give a forceful nudge until attention is focused totally on them. If you are willing, they will climb in your lap and lie contentedly for hours, forgetting they weigh 50 pounds more than the average lap dog. Licking is an annoying habit some Goldens take to extremes, not just with themselves, but humans as well. They will lick the hands or even a face if it is in reach, and delight in covering it with sloppy kisses.

When compared with other breeds, Goldens are considered to be among the most trainable. There are stubborn and slow individuals out there, but even these are seldom hopeless. Most Goldens will learn their basic obedience commands with standard training techniques. They do best if shown what is wanted of them first, rather than being forced into positions. Food treats are a useful motivator to use and hold most Goldens' attention. Yes, Goldens can be easily distracted, as they are often so alert to smells, sights and sounds around them.

Are Goldens Intelligent?

There are many who swear by the intellectual powers of the Golden. The truth is that when rated against other breeds of dogs, Goldens are in the upper middle on the intelligence scale. When we talk about intelligence in dogs, we are referring to the ability to solve problems and quickness in learning tasks. Intelligence is often confused with trainability, which is the Golden's real strength. A dog of average intelligence that wants to please is a good combination.

Golden Retrievers are intelligent and easily trainable dogs.

The Golden's Nose

Especially powerful is the Golden's nose, which often takes over the

Goldens, like all retrievers, take great pleasure in investigating the world with their strong sense of smell.

function of the brain. One of the main reasons hunters have sought Goldens over the years is for their superior scenting ability. The instinct and desire to use their noses to discover and enjoy new and old smells is ever-present in Goldens. On walks or just in their yard, they are constantly on the alert for smells: It is one of the greatest pleasures of their lives.

The retriever part of the dog's name indicates the type of work for which he was developed. It is also an indication that the average Golden with natural instincts is going to spend a good deal of time looking for and carrying any objects he finds in his mouth. Some Goldens are so happy when they have a wonderful object in their mouths they make talking sounds.

Generally Goldens get along well with other domesticated animals. However, as often as we dislike admitting it, they are dogs and exhibit dog-like traits. While it is not a desirable trait, adult males can be aggressive toward other dogs of the same sex. Occasionally females will exhibit the same tendency. Neutering can help control this problem, especially in males. Goldens with prey instinct will chase anything that runs from them, such as cats and rabbits—anything small and fast. Chasing larger animals or livestock is usually not a problem;

they are more likely to bark at larger animals than chase them, though one can never be certain.

Children and Goldens

Children and Goldens would seem a natural pair, and most Goldens delight in the companionship of children. However, one should always take precautions in any situation involving a young child and a dog, even one as gentle in character as a Golden. Some Goldens can be intimidated by boisterous youngsters, while others take them in stride. Some Goldens are too active or possessive of objects to be trusted with children. Children can be accidentally injured by being knocked down or playfully grabbed at. Likewise, a child can hurt a young puppy by rough play.

Friendly to a Fault?

Friendly, outgoing and exuberant in their outlook on life, some Goldens are considered by some to be overly excited or hyper. Due to the very nature of their design, as medium-sized dogs that were bred to work for long periods at a time, they often have a higher level of energy than many breeds. This energy is usually

A Dog's Senses

Sight: Dogs can detect movement at a greater distance than we can, but they can't see as well up close. They can also see better in less light, but they can't distinguish many colors.

Sound: Dogs can hear about four times better than we can, and they can hear high-pitched sounds especially well. Their ancestors, the wolves, howled to let other wolves know where they were; our dogs do the same, but they have a wider range of vocalizations, including barks, whimpers, moans and whines.

Smell: A dog's nose is his greatest sensory organ. His sense of smell is so great he can follow a trail that's weeks old, detect odors diluted to one-millionth the concentration we'd need to notice them, even sniff out a person under water!

Taste: Dogs have fewer taste buds than we do, so they're likelier to try anything—and usually do, which is why it's especially important for their owners to monitor their food intake. Dogs are omnivores, which means they eat meat as well as vegetable matter, like grasses and weeds.

Touch: All dogs are social animals and love to be petted, groomed and played with, especially Goldens.

Goldens generally get along well with other domesticated animals, but sometimes show their prey instinct and chase smaller animals.

easily controlled, and a normal Golden should calm down quickly.

A Golden that is ignored, given little exercise and secluded from attention can develop a behavior that can be described as overexcited. The same dog, if given proper exercise, training and attention, will settle down to a normal level of activity in no time at all.

Certain behaviors should never be tolerated in a Golden. Aggressive actions toward humans, growling, snapping and biting are totally out of character with the breed. The only justification is if circumstances are such that the dog is being hurt or rightfully protecting himself.

Shyness and spookiness are also not in character with the temperament of the Golden. A dog that hides at the sight of visitors or tries to run from anything new can make a satisfactory pet with patience and work. Fearful and aggressive behavior is very easily prevented by early socialization and training. So enroll in puppy classes as early as possible.

Every Golden is a unique individual with slightly different reactions to life. Every one of them has a special trait that distinguishes him from other Golden Retrievers, no matter how many one may have owned. It is safe to say that once a person has owned one, life without a Golden is never the same.

CHAPTER TWO

Homecoming

Before bringing home your new family member, a little planning can help make the transition easier. The first decision to make is where the puppy will live. Will she have access to the entire house or be limited to certain rooms? A similar consideration applies to the yard. It is simpler to control a puppy's activities and to housetrain the puppy if she is confined to definite areas. If doors do not exist where needed, baby gates make satisfactory temporary barriers.

A dog crate is an excellent investment and is an invaluable aid in raising a puppy. It provides a safe, quiet place where a dog can sleep. Used properly, a crate helps with housetraining. The same crate can be used when traveling. A crate that will fit an adult Golden is

Household Dangers

Curious puppies and inquisitive dogs get into trouble not because they are bad, but simply because they want to investigate the world around them. It's our job to protect our dogs from harmful substances, like the following:

In the House

cleaners, especially pine oil

perfumes, colognes, aftershaves

medications, vitamins

office and craft supplies

electric cords

chicken or turkey bones

chocolate

some house and garden plants, like ivy, oleander and poinsettia

In the Garage

antifreeze

garden supplies, like snail and slug bait, pesticides, fertilizers, mouse and rat poisons

approximately 24 inches wide, 36 inches deep and 26 inches high.

Puppy-Proofing

It is definitely easier to raise a puppy than a human baby, but many of the same precautions should be taken. While puppies cannot open cabinets or stick their paws in light sockets, they can get in a lot of trouble with very little effort. Place anything that might be susceptible to puppy teeth or could be broken out of their reach. If possible, all electrical cords should be hidden or secured to floors and walls. Unfortunately such things as tables and chairs cannot be kept out of reach of puppy teeth. If your puppy takes an interest in these, you can buy bitter-tasting sprays to apply to these surfaces.

Puppies may also get into harmful substances. Anything that is poisonous to humans will harm a dog. Antifreeze tastes sweet and is deadly to animals. Most garden sprays, snail baits and rat poisons are toxic to dogs, so they must be kept out of reach and used with extreme caution. Another thing to watch out for are the plants in the yard and in the house.

There are even things that do not bother humans that are dangerous for dogs. Two of these items are chocolate and some salmon. Both are potentially poisonous to dogs and should be kept away from your Golden.

Chew Toys and Accessories

Excessive chewing can be partially resolved by providing a puppy with her own chew toys. Ideal items for Golden pups include stuffed fleece-covered shapes. Goldens love to sink their sharp little teeth into these and carry them around. Braided ropes are fun to pull and shake, and hard rubber balls (never small enough to swallow) are good retrieving objects. It is best to provide a puppy with a few choice toys rather than too many.

As a puppy matures and gets her adult teeth, a variety of items made of hard nylon compounds and in a variety of shapes can provide endless hours of chewing enjoyment. As a Golden ages she will continue to enjoy the toys of puppyhood. Anything given to a dog must be large enough that it cannot be swallowed. Rawhide chews should be given with caution. Some dogs are overzealous in trying to swallow the chewed pieces, and, if large enough, these pieces can get lodged in the throat.

Your puppy will need a close-fitting nylon or cotton-webbed collar. This collar should be adjustable so that it can be used for the first couple of months. A properly fitted collar is tight enough that it will not slip over the head, yet an adult finger fits easily under it. A puppy should never wear a choke chain or any other adult training collar. Even when grown, a dog should only wear a choke chain when she is being trained or under direct supervision.

Puppy-proofing your house before you bring your new dog home will help prevent unfortunate accidents.

In addition to a collar, you'll need a 4-to-6-foot-long leash. One made of nylon or cotton-webbed material is fine as an inexpensive first leash. It need not be more than ½ inch in width. It is important to make sure that the clip is of excellent quality and cannot become unclasped on its own. When a Golden has reached maturity, one may wish to purchase a stronger leash, either of webbed material or leather. Leather is the strongest and will last a long time if properly cared for. The width of the leash should be between 1½ inches and the length between 4 and 6 feet.

The final starter items a puppy will need are a water bowl and food dish. You can select a smaller food dish for your puppy and then get a bigger one when your dog matures. Bowls are available in plastic, stainless steel and even ceramic. Stainless steel is probably the best choice, as it is practically indestructible. Nonspill dishes are available for the dog that likes to play in her water. They are also nearly impossible for a dog to pick up and carry. A 1½-quart bowl is suitable for the amount of food the average Golden might eat at one meal.

Make sure to include a toy or two among the supplies you buy for your puppy's homecoming.

The All-Important Routine

Most puppies do best if their lives follow a schedule. They need definite and regular periods of time for playing, eating and sleeping. Puppies like to start their day early. This is a good time to take a short walk or play some retrieving games. After breakfast, most are ready for a nap. How often this pattern is repeated will depend on one's daily routine. Sometimes it is easier for a working person or family to stick with a regular schedule than it is for someone who is home all of the time.

Most Goldens reach their peak of activity and need the least amount of rest from 6 months to 3 years of age. As they mature they spend increasingly longer periods of time sleeping. It is important to make an effort to ensure that a Golden receives sufficient exercise each day to keep her in proper weight and fitness throughout her life. Puppies need short periods of exercise, but, due to the fact that their bodies are developing, it should never be done to excess. Walks are more suitable for young puppies than running.

Swimming is an excellent exercise and pastime that many Goldens enjoy. If the weather is seasonable and the water warm, they can be introduced to swimming when they're 2 or 3 months old. Some puppies are more willing to enter water if accompanied by a person. Many Goldens will swim after and retrieve sticks out of the water for hours at a time.

Protective Measures

All puppies need some form of identification, even before receiving their rabies shots and being licensed. Most pet stores and veterinary offices have access to sources that make identification tags that can be attached to the puppy's collar. It is more important that the owner's name is on this tag than the dog's name.

Collars and tags have been known to come off and then, suddenly, all means of identification are gone. An additional protection is to have your dog tattooed when she reaches maturity. Your social security number can be used for identification. There are tattoo registries that list dogs. Another form of identification is a microchip, a rice-grain-sized pellet that is actually implanted under the dog's skin. Identification is made by a sensing device. Tattoos and microchips are excellent forms of ID; however, the person who finds a dog may not know to look for a tattoo, and certainly would not know to look for a microchip. Consequently, a dog should wear an ID tag as well as a tattoo or microchip.

Many people find that paper-training their young puppy is a good first step in the housetraining process.

The single best preventative measure one can take to ensure that

Exercise, even in the form of play, is an important aspect of your dog's daily routine.

a dog is not lost or stolen is to provide her with a completely fenced yard. Most Goldens will be contained with a 5-to-6-foot-high fence constructed of wire mesh, chain link or wood. Check the fence periodically for digging spots or weakened structure. While most Goldens are good at staying near their homes, all it takes is one unexpected occurrence for a Golden to be out of her unfenced yard and in potential danger.

CHAPTER THREE

To Good Health

The strongest body and soundest genetic background will not help a dog lead a healthy life unless he receives regular attention from his owner. Dogs are susceptible to infections, parasites and diseases for which they have no natural immunity. It is up to us to take preventative measures to make sure that none of these interferes with our dog's health. It may help to think of the upkeep of a dog's health in relation to the calendar. Certain things need to be done on a weekly, monthly and annual basis.

PREVENTIVE HEALTH CARE

Weekly grooming can be the single best monitor of a dog's overall health. The actual condition of the coat and skin and the "feel" of the body can indicate good health or potential problems. Grooming will help you discover small lumps on or under the skin in the early stages before they become large enough to be seen without close examination.

Run your hands regularly over your dog to feel for any injuries.

You may spot fleas and ticks when brushing the coat and examining the skin. Besides harboring diseases and parasites, they can make daily life a nightmare for some dogs. Many Goldens are severely allergic to even a couple of fleas on their bodies. They scratch, chew and destroy their coat and skin because of fleas.

Flea Control

Flea control is never a simple endeavor. Dogs bring fleas inside, where they lay eggs in the carpeting and furniture—anywhere your dog goes in the house. Consequently, real control is a matter of not only treating the dog but also the other environments the flea inhabits. The yard can be sprayed, and in the house, sprays and flea bombs can be used, but there are more choices for the dog. Flea sprays are effective for one to two weeks. Dips applied to the dog's coat following a bath have equal periods of effectiveness. The disadvantage to both of these is that some dogs may have problems with the chemicals.

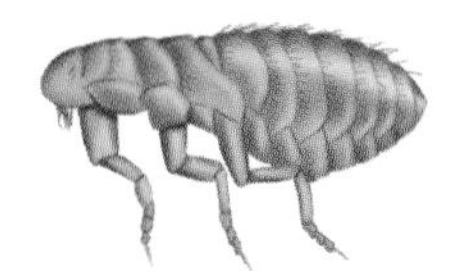

The flea is a die-hard pest.

Flea collars prevent the fleas from traveling to your dog's head, where it's moister and more hospitable. Dog owners tend to leave flea collars on their dogs long after they've ceased to be effective. Again, some dogs may have problems with flea collars, and children should never be allowed to handle them.

Some owners opt for a product that works from the inside out. One such option is a pill (prescribed by a veterinarian) that you give to the dog on a regular basis. The chemicals in the pill course through the dog's bloodstream, and when a flea bites, the blood kills the flea.

Another available option is a product that comes in capsule form. The liquid in the capsule is applied near the dog's shoulders, close to the skin, where it distributes into the skin and coat to protect against fleas and ticks. Ask your veterinarian about this non-toxic, long-lasting flea and tick preventative.

Ticks

As you examine your dog, check also for ticks that may have lodged in his skin, particularly around the ears or in the hair at the base of the ear, the armpits or around the genitals. If you find a tick, which is a small insect about the size of a pencil eraser when engorged with blood, smear it with petroleum jelly. As the tick suffocates, it will back out and you can then grab it with tweezers and kill it. If the tick doesn't back out, grab it with tweezers and slowly pull it out, twisting very gently. Don't just grab and pull or the tick's head may remain in the skin, causing an infection or abscess for which veterinary treatment may be required.

A word of caution: Don't use your fingers or fingernails to pull out ticks. Ticks can carry a number of diseases, including Lyme disease, Rocky Mountain spotted fever and others, all of which can be very serious.

Fighting Fleas

Remember, the fleas you see on your dog are only part of the problem—the smallest part! To rid your dog and home of fleas, you need to treat your dog and your home. Here's how:

- Identify where your pet(s) sleep. These are "hot spots."
- Clean your pets' bedding, your own floors and furniture regularly by vacuuming and washing.
- Spray "hot spots" with a nontoxic, long-lasting flea larvicide.
- Treat outdoor "hot spots" with insecticide.
- Kill eggs on pets with a product containing insect growth regulators (IGRs).
- Kill fleas on pets per your veterinarian's recommendation.

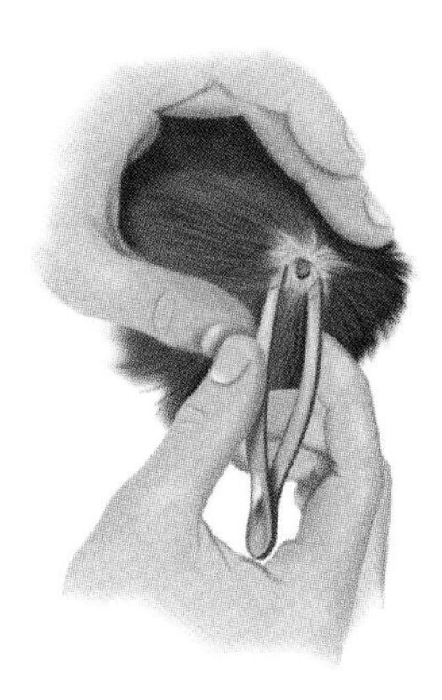

Use tweezers to remove ticks from your dog.

Proper Ear Care

Another weekly job is cleaning the ears. Many times an ear problem is evident if a dog scratches his ears or shakes his head frequently. Clean ears are less likely to develop problems, and if something does occur, it will be spotted while it can be treated easily. If a dog's ears are very dirty and seem to need cleaning on a daily basis, it is a good indication that something else is going on in the ears besides ordinary dirt and the normal accumulation of earwax. A visit to the veterinarian may indicate a situation that needs special medication.

Brushing Teeth

Regular brushing of the teeth often does not seem necessary when a dog is young and spends much of his time chewing; the teeth always seem to be immaculately clean. As a dog ages, it becomes more important to brush the teeth daily.

To help prolong the health of your dog's mouth, he should have his teeth cleaned twice a year at a veterinary clinic. Observing the mouth regularly, checking for the formation of abnormalities or broken teeth, can lead to early detection of oral cancer or infection.

One of the worst enemies of a Golden's teeth is the habit of chewing on his coat. The coarse hairs wear down the front teeth like nothing else he might chew. The only way to prevent this from occurring is to stop the dog from chewing.

Check your dog's teeth frequently and brush them regularly.

Keeping Nails Trimmed

The nails on all feet should be kept short enough so they do not touch the ground when the dog walks.

Dogs with long nails can have difficulty walking on hard or slick surfaces. This can be especially true of older dogs. As nails grow longer, the only way the foot can compensate and retain balance is for the toes themselves to spread apart, causing the foot itself to become flattened and splayed.

Nails that are allowed to become long are also more prone to splitting. This is painful to the dog and usually requires surgical removal of the remainder of the nail for proper healing to occur.

Keeping Eyes Clear

A Golden's eyes rarely need special attention. A small amount of matter in the corner of the eye is normal, as is a bit of "tearing." Goldens with eyelashes that turn inward and rub against the eye itself often exhibit more tearing than normal due to the irritation to the eyes. These eyelashes can be surgically removed if it appears to be a problem, but are often ignored.

Excessive tearing can be an indication that a tear duct is blocked. This, too, can be corrected by a simple surgical procedure. Eye discharge that is thicker and mucous-like in consistency is often a sign of some type of eye infection or actual injury to the eye. This can be verified by a veterinarian, who will provide a topical ointment to place in the corner of the eye. Most minor eye injuries heal quickly if proper action is taken.

VACCINES

All dogs need yearly vaccinations to protect them from common deadly diseases. The DHL vaccine, which protects a dog from distemper, hepatitis and leptospirosis, is given for the first time at about 7 weeks of age, followed by one or two boosters several weeks apart. After this, a dog should be vaccinated every year throughout his life.

Since the mid-1970s, parvovirus and coronavirus have been the cause of death for thousands of dogs. Puppies and older dogs are most frequently affected by these illnesses. Fortunately, vaccines for these are now routinely given on a yearly basis in combination with the DHL shot.

Kennel cough, though rarely dangerous in a healthy dog that receives proper treatment, can be annoying. It can be picked up anywhere that large numbers of dogs congregate, such as veterinary clinics, grooming shops, boarding kennels, obedience classes and dog shows. The Bordatella vaccine, given twice a year, will protect a dog from getting most strains of kennel cough. It is often not routinely given, so it may be necessary to request it.

Internal Parasites

While the exterior part of a dog's body hosts fleas and ticks, the inside of the body is commonly inhabited by a variety of parasites. Most of these are in the worm family. Tapeworms, roundworms, whipworms, hookworms and heartworm all plague dogs. There are also several types of protozoa, mainly *coccidia* and *giardia,* that cause problems.

The common tapeworm is acquired by the dog eating infected fleas or lice. Normally one is not aware that a healthy dog even has tapeworms. The only clues may be a dull coat, a loss of weight despite a good appetite or occasional gastrointestinal problems. Confirmation is by the presence of worm segments in the stool. These appear as small, pinkish-white, flattened rectangular-shaped pieces. When dry, they look like rice. If segments are not present, diagnosis can be made by the discovery of eggs when a stool sample is examined under a microscope. Ridding a dog temporarily of tapeworm is easy with a worming medicine prescribed by a veterinarian. Over-the-counter wormers are not effective for tapeworms and may be dangerous. Long-term tapeworm control is not possible unless the flea situation is also handled.

Common internal parasites (l–r): roundworm, whipworm, tapeworm and hookworm.

Ascarids are the most common roundworm (nematode) found in dogs. Adult dogs that have roundworms rarely exhibit any symptoms that would indicate the worm is in their body. These worms are cylindrical in shape and may be as long as 4 to 5 inches. They do pose a real danger to puppies, where they are usually passed from the mother through the uterus to the unborn puppies.

It is wise to assume that all puppies have roundworms. In heavy infestations they will actually appear in the puppy stools, though their presence is best diagnosed by a stool sample. Treatment is easy and can begin as early as 2 weeks of age and is administered every two weeks thereafter until eggs no longer appear in a stool sample or dead worms are not found in the stool following treatment. Severely infected puppies can die from roundworm infestation. Again, the worming medication should be obtained through a veterinarian.

Hookworm is usually found in warmer climates and infestation is generally from ingestion of larvae from the ground or penetration of the skin by larvae. Hookworms can cause anemia, diarrhea and emaciation. As these worms are very tiny and not visible to the eye, their diagnosis must be made by a veterinarian.

Whipworms live in the large intestine and cause few if any symptoms. Dogs usually become infected when they ingest larvae in contaminated soil. Again, diagnosis and treatment should all be done by a veterinarian. One of the easiest ways to control these parasites is by picking up stools on a daily basis. This will help prevent the soil from becoming infested.

The protozoa can be trickier to diagnose and treat. Coccidiosis and giardia are the most common, and primarily affect young puppies. They are generally associated with overcrowded, unsanitary conditions and can be acquired from the mother (if she is a carrier), the premises themselves (soil) or even water, especially rural puddles and streams.

Your Puppy's Vaccines

Vaccines are given to prevent your dog from getting an infectious disease like canine distemper or rabies. Vaccines are the ultimate preventive medicine. That's why it is necessary for your dog to be vaccinated routinely. Puppy vaccines start at 8 weeks of age for the five-in-one DHLPP vaccine. Your veterinarian will put your puppy on a proper schedule and should remind you when to bring in your dog for shots.

The most common symptom of protozoan infection is mucous-like, blood-tinged feces. It is only with freshly collected samples that diagnosis of this condition can be made. With coccidiosis, besides diarrhea, the puppies will appear listless and lose their appetites. Puppies often harbor the protozoa and show no symptoms unless placed under stress. Consequently, many times a puppy will not become ill until he goes to his new home. Once diagnosed, treatment is quick and effective and the puppy returns to normal almost immediately.

Heartworm

The most serious of the common internal parasites is the heartworm.

A dog that is bitten by a mosquito infected with the heartworm *microfilaria* (larvae) will develop worms that are 6 to 12 inches long. As these worms mature they take up residence in the dog's heart.

The symptoms of heartworm may include coughing, tiring easily, difficulty breathing and weight loss. Heart failure and liver disease may eventually result. Verification of heartworm infection is done by drawing blood and screening for the microfilaria.

In areas where heartworm is a risk, it is best to place a dog on a preventative, usually a pill given once a month.

Depending on where you live, your veterinarian may recommend that your dog be given a monthly heartworm preventative.

At least once a year a dog should have a full veterinary examination. The overall condition of the dog can be observed and a blood sample collected for a complete yearly screening. This way the dog's thyroid functions can be tested, and the job the dog's organs are doing can be monitored. If there are any problems, this form of testing can spot trouble areas while they are easily treatable.

Proper care, regular vaccinations, periodic stool checks and preventative medications for such things as heartworm will all help ensure your dog's health.

Spaying/Neutering

Spaying a female dog or neutering a male is another way to make sure they lead long and healthy lives. Females spayed at a young age have almost no risk of developing mammary tumors or reproductive problems. Neutering a male is an excellent solution to dog aggression and also removes the chances of testicular cancer.

Female Goldens usually experience their first heat cycle somewhere between 6 months and 1 year of age. Unless spayed they will continue to come into heat on a regular cycle.

The length of time between heats varies, with anything from every six months to a year being normal.

There is absolutely no benefit to a female having a first season before being spayed, nor in letting her have a litter. The decision to breed any dog should never be taken lightly. The obvious considerations are whether he or she is a good physical specimen of the breed and has a sound temperament. There are several genetic problems that are common to Goldens, such as hip dysplasia, cataracts, subaortic stenosis (SAS), von Willebrands disease (VWD) and hypothyroidism. Responsible breeders screen for these prior to making breeding decisions.

Finding suitable homes for puppies is another serious consideration. Due to their popularity, many people are attracted to Goldens and seek puppies without realizing the drawbacks of the breed.

Owning a dog is a lifetime commitment to that animal. There are so many unwanted dogs—and yes, even unwanted Goldens—that people must be absolutely sure that they are not just adding to the pet overpopulation problem. When breeding a litter of puppies, it is more likely that you will lose more than you will make, when time, effort, equipment and veterinary costs are factored in.

Advantage of Spaying/Neutering

The greatest advantage of spaying (for females) or neutering (for males) your dog is that you are guaranteed that your dog will not produce puppies. There are too many puppies already available for too few homes. There are other advantages as well.

Advantages of Spaying

No messy heats.

No "suitors" howling at your windows or waiting in your yard.

Prevents pyometra (disease of the uterus) and decreases the incidence of breast cancer.

Advantages of Neutering

Decreases fights, but doesn't affect the dog's personality.

Decreases roaming.

Decreased incidences of urogenital diseases.

Common Problems

Lameness

A limp that appears from nowhere and gets progressively worse is cause for concern. The first thing to do is try to ascertain where the problem actually is. Check the legs and feet for any areas of tenderness, swelling or infection. There are numerous possibilities to consider. In young, developing dogs, lameness in the rear can be an indication of hip dysplasia.

Hip dysplasia is a malformation of the ball and socket joint of the hips and can affect one or both sides of the dog. As a dog ages these joints wear down, and eventually arthritis is associated with the disease. Hip dysplasia can only be properly diagnosed by x-ray.

If x-rays do confirm hip dysplasia, there are several considerations. Surgery is one alternative in more serious cases. In very serious cases the hips themselves are removed and may be replaced with Teflon hips. Most mildly and many moderately dysplastic dogs will lead normal lives if properly managed. A dysplastic dog should be kept in good weight and physical condition. Moderate exercise, especially swimming, is necessary if a dysplastic dog is to lead a normal life. If pain develops with age, it can be relieved with aspirin.

Another common condition that causes lameness in young dogs is osteochondritis dissecans (OCD). This disease affects the shoulder joints and sometimes the hocks and stifles. OCD can be confirmed by

When choosing your puppy, be sure to ask the breeder about the history of hip dysplasia in the puppy's lineage.

x-ray, and the cartilage appears fragmented or loose. In mild cases it will heal itself with rest but usually requires surgery.

Another serious concern with lameness, especially as a dog ages, is bone cancer. This can only be confirmed by tests and x-rays. Anytime a dog or puppy becomes lame and rest is prescribed as treatment, it is essential to keep that dog almost completely inactive, except for potty visits, until the injury heals.

Not Eating or Vomiting

One of the surest signs that a Golden Retriever may be ill is if he does not eat. This is why it is important to know your dog's eating habits. For most dogs one missed meal under normal conditions is not cause for alarm, but more than that and it is time to take your dog to the veterinarian to search for reasons. The vital signs should be checked and gums examined. Normally a dog's gums are pink; if ill they will be pale and gray.

There are many reasons why dogs vomit, and many of them are not cause for alarm. You should be concerned, however, when your dog vomits frequently over the period of a day. If the vomiting is associated with diarrhea, elevated temperature and lethargy, the cause is most likely a virus. The dog should receive supportive veterinary treatment if recovery is to proceed quickly. Vomiting that is not associated with other symptoms is often an indication of an intestinal blockage. Rocks, toys and clothing will lodge in a dog's intestine, preventing the normal passage of digested foods and liquids.

If a blockage is suspected, the first thing to do is an x-ray of the stomach and intestinal region. Sometimes objects will pass on their own, but usually surgical removal of the object is necessary.

Diarrhea

Diarrhea is characterized as very loose to watery stools that a dog has difficulty controlling. It can be caused by anything as simple as changing diet, eating too much food, eating rich human food or having internal parasites.

First try to locate the source of the problem and remove it from the dog's access. Immediate relief is usually available by giving the dog an intestinal relief medication such as

When to Call the Veterinarian

In any emergency situation, you should call your veterinarian immediately. You can make the difference in your dog's life by staying as calm as possible when you call and by giving the veterinarian or the assistant as much information as possible before you leave for the clinic. That way, the staff will be able to take immediate, specific action to remedy your dog's situation.

Emergencies include acute abdominal pain, suspected poisoning, snakebite, burns, frostbite, shock, dehydration, abnormal vomiting or bleeding and deep wounds. You are the best judge of your dog's health, as you live with and observe him every day. Don't hesitate to call your veterinarian if you suspect trouble.

Kaopectate or Pepto-Bismol. Use the same amount per weight as for humans. Take the dog off his food for a day to allow the intestines to rest, then feed meals of cooked rice with bland ingredients added. Gradually add the dog's regular food back into his diet.

If diarrhea is bloody or has a more offensive odor than might be expected and is combined with vomiting and fever, it is most likely a virus and requires immediate veterinary attention. If worms are suspected as the cause, a stool sample should be examined by a veterinarian and treatment to rid the dog of the parasite should follow when the dog is back to normal. If allergies are suspected, a series of tests can be given to find the cause. This is especially likely if, after recovery and no other evidence of a cause exists, a dog returns to his former diet and the diarrhea recurs.

Bloat

Another problem associated with the gastrointestinal system is bloat, or acute gastric dilatation. It most commonly occurs in adult dogs that eat large amounts of dry kibble. Exercise or excessive amounts of water consumed immediately following a meal can trigger the condition.

A dog with bloat will appear restless and uncomfortable. He may drool and attempt to vomit. The abdominal area will appear swollen, and the area will be painful. In severe cases the stomach actually twists on itself and a condition called torsion occurs. If you suspect that your dog is suffering from bloat, run your dog to the nearest veterinary clinic immediately.

Bloat can be prevented by feeding smaller amounts of food several times per day rather than in one large meal. Soaking the food in water prior to feeding it will also help reduce the risk of bloat. Additionally, the dog should be kept from exercising until two or three hours after eating.

Seizures

Seizures vary in severity from trembling and stiffness to frenzied, rapid movements of the legs, foaming at the mouth and loss of urine and bowel movements. The latter is usually considered a grand mal seizure.

Seizures are caused by electrical activity in the brain, and there are many reasons why they may occur. Ingestion of some poisons, such as strychnine and insecticides, will cause seizures. These are generally long lasting and severe in nature. Injuries to the skull, tumors and cancers can trigger seizures.

If there appears to be no reason for the seizure it is possible the cause is congenital epilepsy. This is particularly true if a dog is under the age of 3. From the age of 5, dogs are prone to develop old age onset epilepsy, which also may have a genetic predisposition.

Never try to touch or move a dog during a seizure. If there is anything nearby that might be knocked over by their flailing legs and injure them, move it out of the way. If the seizure does not stop within five minutes, call your veterinarian.

Even after a typical seizure, your vet may suggest you bring your dog in for an examination and blood work. If a cause is not found, the best course is usually to wait and see if your dog has another seizure. If a dog only has seizures once or twice a year there is no reason to place him on preventive medication. If seizures occur on a regular basis and are of the same nature each time, the dog is considered to have epilepsy and medication should be considered.

In typical epilepsy, the dog may act restless, weird, stare and bark for some time before the actual seizure. The seizure itself lasts several minutes. A second seizure can be triggered by turning a light on or by moving the dog as he is recovering.

If seizures are infrequent and mild, an epileptic dog can lead a fairly normal life. Owners will generally begin to see a pattern in the

Identify Your Dog

It is a terrible thing to think about, but your dog could somehow, someday, get lost or stolen. How would you get him back? Your best bet would be to have some form of identification on your dog. You can choose from a collar and tags, a tattoo, a microchip or a combination of these three.

Every dog should wear a buckle collar with identification tags. They are the quickest and easiest way for a stranger to identify your dog. It's best to inscribe the tags with your name and phone number; you should not include your dog's name.

There are two ways to permanently identify your dog. The first is a tattoo, placed on the inside of your dog's thigh. The tattoo should be your social security number or your dog's AKC registration number.

The second is a microchip, a rice-sized pellet that is inserted under the dog's skin at the base of the neck, between the shoulder blades. When a scanner is passed over the dog, it will beep, notifying the person that the dog has a chip. The scanner will then show a code, identifying the dog. Microchips are becoming more and more popular and are certainly the wave of the future.

time of day the seizures occur and their frequency, and can plan their dog's activities accordingly.

Coughing

Throughout the day most dogs will cough to get something out of their throats and it is usually ignored. If coughing persists, then it is time to look for causes.

A common cause for a dry hacking cough is kennel cough, which is contagious and usually picked up through association with other dogs. A dog with kennel cough should receive veterinary attention and be placed on antibiotics and a cough suppressant. During treatment and recovery, the dog should be kept indoors and warm as much as possible. Kennel cough, if not cared for properly, can easily turn into pneumonia in cold conditions. Infected dogs should be isolated from other dogs until they have recovered.

Chronic coughing after exercise can also be a sign of heart failure, especially in an older dog. It may also indicate a heartworm infection. If this occurs regularly, consult your veterinarian.

Most changes in the breathing pattern of a healthy dog, such as rapid inhalations or panting, are caused by exercise, stress and heat. If a dog is having problems breathing and it is also accompanied by coughing or gagging, it may be a sign that an air passage is blocked. Check for an object lodged in your dog's throat. If you can't remove it yourself, use the Heimlich maneuver. Place your dog on his side and, using both hands palms down, apply quick thrusts to the abdomen, just below the dog's last rib. If your dog won't lie down, grasp either side of the end of the rib cage and squeeze in short thrusts. Make a sharp enough movement to cause the air in the lungs to force the object out. If the cause cannot be found or removed, then professional help is needed.

Shallow breathing can be a result of an injury to the ribs or a lung problem. A wheezing noise that can be heard as a dog breathes is an indication of a serious problem. If other symptoms include a fever and lethargy, the problem may be associated with a lung disease. The symptoms may indicate treatment for an infection. An x-ray can confirm the presence of a growth or infection in the lungs.

Sometimes a dog exhibits no greater signs that something is different than increased lethargy, weight gain and even a poor coat. It may be time to consider checking the dog's thyroid levels for a possible hypothyroid condition. Low thyroid most commonly results in a poor coat and skin and eventual infertility in an intact male or female. A thyroid test will indicate what levels of the function of the thyroid are low and whether daily thyroid medication should be given.

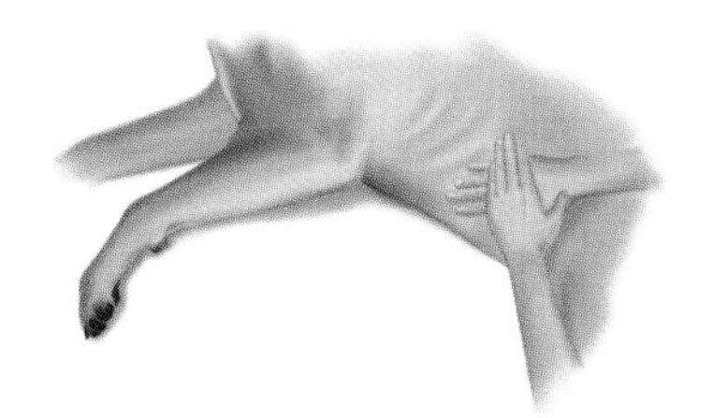

Applying abdominal thrusts can save a choking dog.

Skin Problems

Certain skin conditions should not be ignored if home treatment is not working. For example, if a dog is so sensitive and allergic to fleas that his coat and skin are literally destroyed by chewing, it is time to seek help. Cortisone can help relieve the itching and stop the dog from destroying himself, but it has side effects, too! It's best to get your vet's advice.

Mange is caused by tiny mites that live on the dog's skin. The most common types are sarcoptic and demodetic mange. Diagnosis must be made by a veterinarian, since the mites are too small to be seen.

Sarcoptic mange first occurs as small red bumps on the dog's skin and causes intense itching. If allowed to continue there is hair loss from chewing, and the affected skin becomes crusty, especially around the muzzle, elbows and hocks.

The mite that causes demodetic mange lives in the pores of the skin of most dogs. Certain conditions cause the dog's natural immunity to this mite to break down, and the result is patches of hair loss, usually around the nose or eyes. There is no itching associated with this condition and it primarily occurs in dogs under 1 year of age. If treated properly the hair returns to normal. In the generalized form of the disease, hair loss occurs in large patches all over the body. Obviously this is a much more serious condition.

Hot spots are one of the most baffling skin problems. They can be caused by a number of things, including flea bites and allergies. A warm, moist, infected area on the skin appears out of nowhere and can be several inches large. At home one should clip the hair around it, then clean it with an antiseptic and dilute (3 percent hydrogen peroxide). Spraying with a topical anaesthetic immediately relieves itching. Topical ointments can also help. If the spot is not healing and appears to be getting larger or infected, veterinary help should be sought.

A similar type of skin condition is the lick sore. These sores are almost always on the lower part of the front legs or tops of the feet. A dog will lick a spot and out of boredom continue licking it until the hair is gone and the skin is hard, red and shiny. The sore will heal on its own if kept clean and the dog is prevented access to it by an anti-chewing spray or by wearing an Elizabethan collar.

Tumors

As dogs age they are more apt to develop various types of tumors. Fatty tumors grow just under the dog's skin and are not attached to anything. These are usually benign accumulations of fatty cells. If you see or feel any such lumps on your dog, you should consult your veterinarian. Tumors and bumps that appear and grow rapidly, are strange in color or appearance or are attached to the bone should receive immediate attention.

Cuts and Wounds

Any cut over 1/2 inch in length should be stitched for it to heal. Small cuts usually heal by themselves if they are rinsed well, washed with an antibiotic soap and checked regularly with further cleansing of soap or a hydrogen peroxide solution. When they occur in areas that are exposed to dirt, such as the feet, it may be advisable to place a wrap on the injury, but it should be removed frequently. If signs of infection appear, such as swelling, redness or warmth, it should be looked at by a veterinarian.

Puncture wounds should never be bandaged or stitched. They occur most commonly from bites, nails or wires. Anytime it is suspected that a dog might have been pierced by a nail or bitten, the body should be carefully examined for such wounds. As they often do not bleed very much they can be difficult to spot. If not treated, they can result in infection or even conditions as dangerous as tetanus.

If the wound is discovered within a short time of the occurrence, try to make it bleed by applying pressure around it. Flush it with water, then clean it with soap. Leave it exposed so that oxygen is able to stay in the wound and prevent an anaerobic condition from developing. Place a dilute hydrogen peroxide on it several times a day. Watch it carefully for any indications of infection. Anytime your dog is injured, consider placing him on an antibiotic to prevent infection.

An Elizabethan collar keeps your dog from licking a fresh wound.

GIVING MEDICATION

When a dog has been diagnosed with a problem that requires medication it is usually in the form of a pill or liquid. Because it is essential for a dog to have the entire pill or capsule in order for the dosage to be effective, it's necessary to actually give the dog the pill rather than mix it in his food or wrap it in meat,

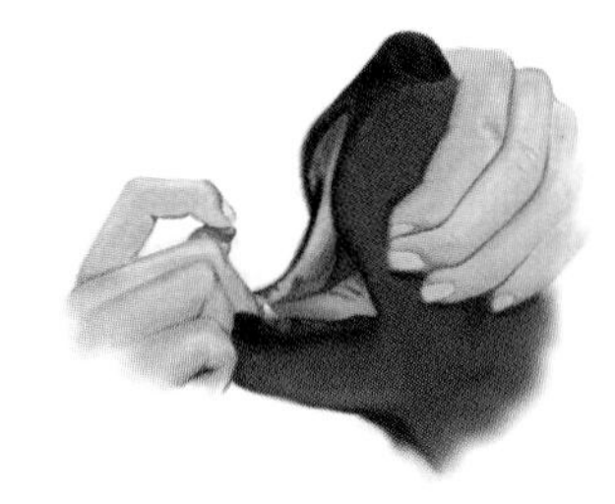

To give a pill, open the mouth wide, then drop it in the back of the throat.

which can be chewed up and spit out. Open your dog's mouth and place the pill on the back of the middle of his tongue. Then hold his head up with his mouth held shut and stroke his throat. When the dog swallows, you can let go.

Liquid medication is most easily given in a syringe. These are usually marked so the amount is accurately measured. Hold the dog's head upward at about 45°, open the mouth slightly and place the end of the syringe in the area in the back of the mouth between the cheek and rear molars. Hold your dog's mouth shut until he swallows.

If your dog needs eye medication, apply it by pulling down the lower eyelid and placing the ointment on the inside of the lid. Then close the eye and gently disperse the solution around the eye. Eye drops can be placed directly on the eye. Giving ear medicine is similar to cleaning the ears. The drops are placed in the canal and the ear is then massaged.

Squeeze eye ointment into the lower lid.

Common Golden Retriever Problems

Cataracts—There are several types of cataracts that affect Goldens. They are characterized by the part of the lens on which they appear and the age of the dog. Most are genetic, though others can be caused by injury or the aging process. Most cataracts are nonprogressive in Goldens and impairment of vision is usually mild. Diagnosis must be made by a veterinary ophthalmologist.

Epilepsy—Genetic epilepsy usually appears prior to 3 years of age. The old age onset form may have a genetic predisposition. These are seizures that occur regularly and follow a typical pattern. Epilepsy can be controlled by daily medication.

Hip Dysplasia—Genetic and environmental in origin, it is the malformation of the ball and socket joints of the hips. Severe forms cause lameness and may require surgery. Diagnosis is only by x-ray.

Low Thyroid (Hypothyroidism)—It may be genetic and is also associated with poor immunity. There may be physical signs, such as weight gain, lethargy, poor coat, infertility in both sexes and longer than normal periods of time between heat cycles. A thyroid test will indicate if there is a problem. Daily medication will correct the thyroid levels and return a dog to normal.

Lymphosarcoma—This form of cancer, which affects the lymph system, is becoming alarmingly common in many related and unrelated families of Goldens. Symptoms may include poor appetite, lethargy and chronically swollen lymph nodes. Treatment can prolong a dog's life for as much as a year. Dogs may be genetically predisposed to it, and it is linked to autoimmune problems.

Osteochondritis Dissecans (OCD)—There appears to be a genetic predisposition to malformation of the cartilage of the long bones that subsequently results in the injury of that cartilage. This can be treated by rest in minor cases or surgery. X-rays verify this condition.

Progressive Retinal Atrophy (PRA)—This is less common in Goldens than cataracts, but it still occurs. PRA is a gradual degeneration of the cells of the retina. It first occurs in middle-aged dogs and leads to loss of vision. Diagnosis is the same as for cataracts. CERF (Canine Eye Registry Foundation) was established to benefit breeding programs by registering dogs whose eyes test free of genetic problems.

Skin Allergies and Hot Spots—A genetic predisposition to skin allergies may exist. The thick undercoat, especially if it stays damp, is an excellent environment for the development of hot spots.

Subaortic Stenosis (SAS)—This is a genetically caused defect in the valve ring below the aorta of the heart. It is detected by a murmur, and accurate diagnosis is made by a variety of advanced techniques including auscultation and echo-cardiogram. In cases of minor murmurs a dog should lead a normal, though sedate, life. Dogs with severe grades of SAS will show physical signs and often die unexpectedly at a young age. Diagnosis should be made by a registered canine cardiologist.

VON WILLEBRANDS DISEASE—A genetic bleeding disorder that might be suspected if it takes longer than normal for a wound to stop bleeding. Other indications are high mortality rates in newborn puppies or poor fertility in a female. A blood specimen treated and tested at a specially equipped facility is necessary to diagnose this disease.

FIRST AID AND EMERGENCIES

While we never plan on emergencies happening, we can be partially prepared by knowing which veterinary clinics are open if something occurs at night or on the weekend. Telephone numbers should be posted so they can be easily located.

First-aid measures can be taken to help ensure that your dog gets to a veterinarian in time for treatment to be effective.

Anytime a dog is in extreme pain, even the most docile one may bite if touched. As a precaution, the dog's mouth should be restrained with some type of muzzle. A rope, pair of pantyhose or strip of cloth about 2 feet long all work in a pinch.

First tie a loose knot that has an opening large enough to easily fit around the dog's nose. Once it is on, tighten the knot on the top of the muzzle. Then bring the two ends down and tie another knot underneath the dog's chin. Finally, pull the ends behind the head and tie a knot below the ears. Don't do this if there is an injury to the head or the dog requires artificial respiration.

If a dog has been injured or is too ill to walk on his own he will

Use a scarf or old hose to make a temporary muzzle, as shown.

have to be carried to be moved. It is important to be very careful when this is done to prevent further injury or trauma. Keep the dog's body as flat and still as possible. Two people are usually needed to move a large dog. A blanket can work if all four corners are held taut. A piece of plywood or extremely stiff cardboard works best, if available.

Artificial Respiration—Artificial respiration is necessary if breathing has stopped. Situations that may cause a state of unconsciousness include drowning, choking, electric shock or even shock itself. If you've taken a course in human CPR you will discover that similar methods are used on dogs. The first thing to do is check the mouth and air passages for any object that might obstruct breathing. If you find nothing, or when it is cleared, hold the dog's mouth while covering the nose completely with your mouth. Gently exhale into the dog's nose. This should be done at between ten to twelve breaths per minute.

If the heart has stopped beating, place the dog on his right side and place the palm of your hand on the rib cage just behind the elbows. Press down six times and then wait

A First-Aid Kit

Keep a canine first-aid kit on hand for general care and emergencies. Check it periodically to make sure liquids haven't spilled or dried up, and replace medications and materials after they're used. Your kit should include:

- Activated charcoal tablets
- Adhesive tape (1 and 2 inches wide)
- Antibacterial ointment (for skin and eyes)
- Aspirin (buffered or enteric coated, not Ibuprofen or acetaminophen)
- Bandages: gauze rolls (1 and 2 inches wide) and dressing pads
- Cotton balls
- Diarrhea medicine
- Dosing syringe
- Hydrogen peroxide (3%)
- Petroleum jelly
- Rectal thermometer
- Rubber gloves
- Rubbing alcohol
- Scissors
- Tourniquet
- Towel
- Tweezers

A healthy Golden is a happy Golden.

five seconds and repeat. This should be done in conjunction with artificial respiration, so it will require two people. Artificial respiration should be continued until the dog breathes on his own or the heart beats. Heart massage should continue until the heart beats on its own or no beat is felt for five minutes.

Shock—Whenever a dog is injured or is seriously ill, the odds are good that he will go into a state of shock. A dog in shock will be listless, weak and cold to the touch. His gums will be pale. If not treated, a dog will die from shock, even if the illness or injuries themselves are not fatal. The conditions of the dog should continue to be treated, but the dog should be kept as comfortable as possible. A blanket can help keep the dog warm. A dog in shock needs immediate veterinary care.

Severe Bleeding—When severe bleeding from a cut occurs the area should be covered with bandaging material or a clean cloth and should have pressure applied to it. If it appears that an artery is involved and the wound is on a limb, then a tourniquet should be applied. This can be made of a piece of cloth, gauze or sock if nothing else is available. It should be tied above the wound and checked every few minutes to make sure it is not so tight that circulation to the rest of the limb is cut off.

Fracture—If a fracture is felt or suspected, the dog should be moved and transported as carefully as possible to a veterinarian.

Poisoning—In the case of poisoning the only thing to do is get help immediately. If you know the source of the poison, take the container or object with you, as this may aid treatment.

In acidic or alkaline poisonings the chemicals must be neutralized. Pepto-Bismol or milk of magnesia at 2 teaspoons per 5 pounds of weight can be given for acids. Vinegar diluted at one part to four parts water at the same dosage can relieve alkaline poisons.

Some of the many household substances harmful to your dog.

HEATSTROKE—Heatstroke occurs when a dog's body temperature greatly exceeds the normal 101.5°F. It can be caused by overexercise in warm temperatures, or if a dog is left in a closed vehicle for any period of time. A dog should *never* be left in an unventilated, unshaded vehicle.

Dogs suffering from heatstroke will feel hot to the touch and inhale short, shallow, rapid breaths. The heartbeat will be very fast. The dog must be cooled immediately, preferably being wet down with cool water in any way that is available. The dog should be wrapped in cool, damp towels and taken to the veterinarian immediately.

The opposite of heatstroke is hypothermia. When a dog is exposed to extreme cold for long periods of time his body temperature drops, he becomes chilled and he can go into shock. The dog should be placed in a warm environment and wrapped in towels or blankets. Massaging the body will help increase the circulation to normal levels.

Insect Bites

The seriousness of reactions to insect bites varies. The affected area will be red, swollen and painful. In the case of bee stings the stinger should always be removed. A paste made of baking soda and water can be applied to the wound and ice applied to the area for the relief of swelling. The bites of some spiders, centipedes and scorpions can cause severe illness and lead to shock.

CHAPTER FOUR

Positively Nutritious

The nutritional needs of a dog will change throughout her lifetime. It is necessary to be aware of these changes not only for proper initial growth to occur, but also so your dog can lead a healthy life for many years.

When a puppy first leaves the home of her breeder, she should have been weaned from her dam for at least one week and should be eating puppy food. Be sure to ask what type of puppy food that is and plan on continuing to use it for at least the first few days your puppy is in her new home. If it's a premium dog food and is readily available where you live, there is no reason not to continue feeding it. If for some reason you wish to switch food, then do so gradually. Ask the breeder to give you several days' supply and gradually mix it in with the new food.

Life-Stage Feeding

Puppies and adolescent dogs require a much higher intake of protein, calories and nutrients than adult dogs due to the demands of their rapidly developing bodies. Most commercial brands of dry kibble meet these requirements and are well balanced for proper growth. Adding supplements to a well-formulated dog food will destroy the designed balance. For example, the addition of calcium can lead to improper bone growth and result in structural problems. The majority of puppy foods now available are so carefully planned that it is unwise to attempt to add anything other than water to them.

The major ingredients of most dry dog foods are chicken, beef or lamb by-products and corn, wheat or rice. The higher the meat content, the greater the protein percentage, palatability and digestibility of the food. Protein percentages in puppy food are usually between 25 and 40 percent. There are many advantages of dry dog foods over semimoist and canned dog foods for puppies and normal, healthy adult Goldens.

The two best reasons to feed dry food are:

1. The chewing action involved in eating a dry food is better for the health of the teeth and gums.

2. Dry food is less expensive than canned food of equal quality.

Dogs whose diets are based on canned or soft foods have a greater likelihood of developing calcium deposits and gum disease. Canned or semimoist foods do serve certain functions, however. As a supplement to dry dog food, in small portions, canned or semimoist foods can be useful to stimulate appetites and increase needed weight gain. But unless very special conditions exist they are not the best way for a dog to meet her food needs.

Your Puppy's Meal Plan

A Golden puppy should be fed three times a day until she is 6 months old. How these feedings are spaced out during the day will depend on

The action of chewing dry food helps maintain the health of your dog's teeth and gums.

Goldens are frequently extra-eager eaters, so you should keep an eye out for excessive weight gain.

one's schedule. There is no set rule on the quantity of food to feed.

As Goldens can often be big eaters, it is easy for them to become overweight. There is a fine line between proper growth and excessive weight. The ribs or bones of a puppy should never protrude or be visible. This is a sign that nutritional needs are not being met. Though not visible, when hands are placed on the body of the pup, those ribs should be easy to feel. If the hands sink into the body, then the food amounts should be cut back.

A good plan to follow is to divide the amount recommended by the veterinarian by three. If the puppy is finishing all three of these portions throughout the day and the appearance of the body indicates proper growth, then stay with those amounts. If the puppy looks like she is gaining weight excessively, then reduce the amount that is given. The same applies for the puppy that leaves quantities of food uneaten, yet is at a good weight and energy level otherwise. Obviously if a puppy is eating her rations and appears thin, her food intake should be increased. This is something that can only be accomplished by observation and good judgment.

There are Golden pups that could not care less for food. They are more interested in other activities than eating. They will finally eat when it is absolutely necessary, but the result is slower than normal growth and a thin appearance. Sometimes these pups can be taught to appreciate food by the addition of a small amount of canned dog food. Regular meals build an appetite and develop the habit of eating normally.

While the food does not need to soak in water, the addition of a small amount of water will increase the palatability of the food. Some studies have shown that soaking food for a short period of time prior to being fed increases its digestibility and lessens the chances of gastric disorders such as bloat.

Puppies and dogs should have a place of their own where they can eat their meals without disturbance. A dog crate can be an ideal place to feed a dog. If a household consists of more than one dog, it is a wise idea to feed the dogs separately. More dog fights occur over food rights than any other issue. Give a dog a definite period of time to eat her food rather than allowing her to nibble throughout the day. If the food has not been eaten within a ten-minute period, pick it up and do not feed again until the next mealtime. One of the best ways to spot health problems in dogs, and Goldens in particular because they tend to be such good eaters, is monitoring their food intake. Most Goldens that miss a meal under normal circumstances are not well.

Some owners like to spice up their dogs' lives with human food. Scraps given regularly can lead to weight gain if the amount of the dog's regular food is not reduced. The risk of destroying the nutritional balance of the dog food also exists. Some human foods fed in large quantities can lead to gastrointestinal problems, which can result in loose stools and even diarrhea.

From 6 months to 1 year of age the puppy should remain on puppy

To Supplement or Not to Supplement?

If you're feeding your dog a diet that's correct for her developmental stage and she's alert, healthy-looking and neither over- nor underweight, you don't need to add supplements. These include table scraps as well as vitamins and minerals. In fact, a growing puppy is in danger of developing musculoskeletal disorders by oversupplementation. If you have any concerns about the nutritional quality of the food you're feeding, discuss them with your veterinarian.

Once your Golden reaches the age of 8 or 9, it is wise to begin feeding her a food with a reduced fat and protein content.

While you may be tempted to add scraps from your dinner plate to your dog's food bowl, these extra treats can lead to unwanted weight gain.

food, but the feedings should decrease to twice a day. By the time a dog reaches 1 year of age she should be switched to an adult maintenance diet. The number of feedings can remain at twice a day, though it is easier for most owners to feed a large meal once a day. A dog that is prone to digestive problems may be better off with two smaller meals.

If a dog is very active, a canine athlete, so to speak, one may want to use a food with a higher protein content than normal, 28 percent for example. As dogs mature and slow down they no longer have the protein or caloric needs of younger dogs. The ingredients of the food should reflect these changes.

Some dogs are allergic to certain grains and meats and this will directly affect what they can eat. Such allergies are indicated by skin problems or an inability to properly digest the food. This can be confirmed by veterinary tests. Lamb- and rice-based foods are considered to be the least allergenic and most easily digestible for dogs with allergies to other food sources.

The amount of food an adult Golden should eat daily will vary according to the size of the dog, her activity level and how much time she spends outside.

Most Golden owners should consider placing their dog on a food that is very low in fat and protein content by the age of 8 or 9, unless the dog is still very active. A dog that is inactive either by choice or the owner's laziness has lower nutritional requirements. Another thing to keep in mind is that as dogs age, their kidneys can be destroyed if kept on a food with a high protein content. Foods formulated for older dogs are low in fat and protein content (as low as 8 percent and below 18 percent in protein).

Maintaining the proper weight and nutrition of an older Golden is probably more difficult than at any other stage of life. A certain amount of body fat is necessary to protect her in the event of illness. Too much excess weight will make the dog even less active and more prone to physical problems. If a dog develops such problems as kidney failure, heart disease or an overly sensitive digestive tract, there are specially formulated foods commercially available.

The physical appearance a Golden presents is as much a result of genetics as it is the food she eats. The owner that feeds a high quality food and keeps her in optimum weight for her size will be rewarded with a Golden whose health and fitness mirrors her diet.

How to Read the Dog Food Label

With so many choices on the market, how can you be sure you're feeding the right food for your dog? The information's all there on the label—if you know what you're looking for. Look for the nutritional claim right up top. Is the food "100% nutritionally complete?" If so, it's for nearly all life stages; "growth and maintenance," on the other hand, is for early development; puppy foods are marked as such, as are foods for senior dogs.

Ingredients are listed in descending order by weight. The first three or four ingredients will tell you the bulk of what the food contains. Look for the highest-quality ingredients, like meats and grains, to be among them.

The guaranteed analysis tells you what levels of protein, fat, fiber and moisture are in the food, in that order. While these numbers are meaningful, they won't tell you much about the quality of the food. Nutritional value is in the dry matter, not the moisture content.

In many ways, seeing is believing. If your dog has bright eyes, a shiny coat, a good appetite and a good energy level, chances are her diet's fine. Golden Retrievers rarely skip their meals.

CHAPTER FIVE

Putting on the Dog

As a breed, Goldens require a minimum amount of regular grooming to remain clean and attractive. A little brushing, an occasional bath and a bit of trimming pretty much cover the needs of a Golden.

Grooming should begin while a dog is a puppy and should become routine. Some breeders clip puppy nails weekly until they go to their new homes. This teaches the puppy to accept having his nails clipped. Some breeders also use a fine-toothed comb daily to remove dirt from the coats. Mouths and baby teeth are checked to see how bites are developing, and ears are observed for cleanliness. All of these preliminary steps taken by the breeder will help make grooming easier for the new owner as long as the process is continued.

Getting Started

For starters, one will need a small slicker brush and a fine-toothed comb. When a puppy is young it is a good idea to brush and/or comb him daily. If a puppy is not already used to having his nails clipped it is best to start this now rather than waiting and battling a 70-pound dog. Human nail clippers can be used on puppies until they are about 3 months old. These make it easier to remove just the tips of tiny nails. Be sure to clip the dewclaws if these have not been removed.

Check your Golden's ears regularly, and even if they do not look dirty, get him used to having a cotton swab soaked in a little ear cleaner run around the inside of the ear. Lift up your dog's lips and inspect the mouth. Your puppy will become used to being examined and having sensitive parts of his body handled, and you will learn what is normal for your dog, making it easier to spot potential problems before they require more serious attention.

How much coat care the adult Golden requires will depend on the type of coat he carries. A heavily coated dog with lots of feathering will need more upkeep than a dog with less coat and sparse feathers. A Golden should have at least one session of brushing per week, but some circumstances require more frequent care. All kinds of brushes, shedders and matt splitters are available, but all that is really needed is a large slicker brush and a comb. Areas that require special attention are the feathers of the front and rear legs, the tail feathers and the fine hair just

Cleaning your dog's ears is easy—just run a moistened cotton ball along the inside ear flap and avoid cleaning into the ear canal.

Combing your Golden will be especially important during heavy shedding periods.

underneath and behind the ears. All of these areas are prone to matting due to scratching, chewing or things getting caught in the longer hair.

Goldens shed their coats twice a year. When this occurs will depend on the climate in your area. When your dog sheds, his fine undercoat is lost *en masse,* often in clumps. During periods of shedding, you may wish to brush your dog several times a day to keep the fine undercoat from ending up all over the house and yard.

You can help loosen up the coat by running your hands and fingers through it, massaging the skin. Some say this helps stimulate new coat growth. Regardless, it helps to speed the shedding process and is enjoyable for the dog.

Taking a Bath

Goldens should be bathed no more than every six to eight weeks, and even this may be unnecessary on a shorter-coated dog that swims frequently. Certain skin conditions may warrant more frequent bathing with specially treated or medicated shampoos. Excessive bathing can destroy the natural balance of oils of your Golden's skin and coat.

Human shampoos should never be used on dogs. They are formulated for the pH of human hair and skin, which is quite different from that of a dog. There are many shampoos available that are specifically designed for dogs. If in doubt as to what to use, call a grooming shop and find out what they recommend.

Prior to bathing a dog be sure he is well brushed and free of matts. Matts left in the coat will become even tighter and harder to remove if they go through the bathing process. Baths work best if lukewarm water is used; however, cold water is fine if the weather is warm. Wet the dog thoroughly and then apply the shampoo, making sure to keep it out of the eyes and ears. You can put cotton balls in the ears to keep excess water out. When rinsing, be sure to get all the soap out. Keep rinsing even after all of the soap appears to be gone. Soap left on the dog can irritate his skin.

If the dog is being washed with a flea shampoo, remember that the suds will need to sit on the dog for several minutes before they are rinsed off. A flea shampoo only kills the fleas that are on the dog at the time he is being bathed. Once it is rinsed off, the fleas will be back on the dog. If a flea dip is applied it should be done after the soap has been rinsed out. Flea dips are only effective if a dog is clean.

After his bath, towel your dog off to remove excess water. Most Goldens will shake wildly at some time during and after the bath and get you completely wet. If it is a warm day a dog can be left to dry on his own; in colder weather use a handheld hair dryer set at low heat.

Grooming Tools

- pin brush
- slicker brush
- flea comb
- towel
- matt rake
- grooming glove
- clippers
- scissors
- nail clippers
- tooth-cleaning equipment
- shampoo
- conditioner

A bath every two months or so will keep your Golden looking his best.

Don't Neglect Nails

Trimming nails is essential for the well-being of your dog's feet. Dogs that receive lots of exercise or that are on cement may wear their nails down enough on their own that clipping is unnecessary. But even these dogs, as they become older and less active, will need nail care. Normally, nails should be trimmed every two weeks or when the nails start to touch the floor. This is

The most important thing to remember when trimming your Golden's nails is not to cut too much and nick the quick.

noticeable as a clicking sound when the dog walks on hard surfaces.

Besides large-sized nail clippers, you should buy styptic powder specifically for dog nails. Keep it on hand in case you cut a nail too short. The blood vessel in a nail is referred to as the quick and serves as the blood supply to the nail. If the tip of the quick is cut, it will bleed. To be safe, only cut the hook part of the nail until you're more confident. Most of the time a minor cut to the quick will stop bleeding on its own. The styptic powder will stop the bleeding; if it doesn't, applying the powder along with some pressure does the job.

If clipping nails is a scary proposition for you, most groomers and veterinary clinics will take care of it for a small fee.

Caring for Ears and Teeth

Your Golden's ears will need weekly cleaning. Even if they do not appear dirty, frequent care will prevent ear problems. Ear-cleaning solutions are available in pet stores. Place several drops in each ear and massage the ears for half a minute. This way the solution can penetrate the greasy dirt. Let the dog shake his head to loosen the dirt. To actually remove the dirt, use cotton swabs or cotton balls. Clean the exterior areas of the inside of the ear, getting into the nooks and crannies of the outer ear. A need for more frequent cleanings may require veterinary attention.

We rarely think about the cleanliness of our dogs' teeth, leaving that to the natural cleansing action of chewing. However, dogs develop gum disease and tooth degeneration just like humans. We can help counter this progression by brushing the teeth regularly. Canine toothpastes and toothbrushes are available and can be used daily.

CHAPTER SIX

Measuring Up

WHAT IS A BREED STANDARD?

A breed standard—a detailed description of an individual breed—is meant to portray the *ideal* specimen of that breed. This includes ideal structure, temperament, gait and type—all aspects of the dog. Because the standard describes an ideal specimen, it isn't based on any particular dog. It is a concept against which judges compare actual dogs and breeders strive to produce dogs. At a dog show, the dog that wins is the one that comes closest, in the judge's opinion, to the standard for her breed.

The overall appearance of the Golden Retriever is described in the opening paragraph of the breed's official American Kennel Club "breed standard," which was revised and adopted in 1982. The Golden should be an athletic dog whose overall attitude is as much a part of her "being" as any physical

The American Kennel Club

Familiarly referred to as "the AKC," the American Kennel Club is a nonprofit organization devoted to the advancement of purebred dogs. The AKC maintains a registry of recognized breeds and adopts and enforces rules for dog events including shows, obedience trials, field trials, hunting tests, lure coursing, herding, earthdog trials, agility and the Canine Good Citizen program. It is a club of clubs, established in 1884 and composed, today, of over 500 autonomous dog clubs throughout the United States. Each club is represented by a delegate; the delegates make up the legislative body of the AKC, voting on rules and electing directors. The American Kennel Club maintains the Stud Book, the record of every dog ever registered with the AKC, and publishes a variety of materials on purebred dogs, including a monthly magazine, books and numerous educational pamphlets.

components. It is important to keep in mind when reading the standard and trying to match one's own Golden to it that the standard describes an *ideal* Golden, and some sections are geared toward a show interpretation.

What follow are descriptions of the ideal Golden Retriever. Excerpts from the breed standard appear in italics, and are followed by an explanation of their statements.

General Appearance

A symmetrical, powerful, active dog, sound and well put together, not clumsy nor long in the leg, displaying a kindly expression and possessing a personality that is eager, alert and self-confident. Primarily a hunting dog, she should be shown in hard working condition. Overall appearance, balance, gait and purpose to be given more emphasis than any of her component parts.

Size

Males 23–24 inches in height at the withers; females $21\frac{1}{2}$ *to* $22\frac{1}{2}$ *inches. Dogs up to one inch above or below standard should be proportionately penalized. Deviation in height of more than one inch from the standard shall disqualify. Length from breastbone to point of buttocks slightly greater than height at withers in ratio of 12:11. Weight for dogs 65–75 pounds; bitches 55–65 pounds.*

Measuring Height

The standard Golden is a medium-sized dog. Measuring a dog's height is done by using a yardstick and a flat surface (for example, a sheet of cardboard) that is gently placed at the flat area where the neck and back meet (the withers; see tear card for illustration of the parts of the body). A Golden's height may vary an inch over or under and remain within the standard. The Golden should be slightly longer in body than height. The weight recommendations are meant for dogs of proper height that are in working condition. Obviously, an overweight dog will not fall within these weights. The tendency for Goldens to be larger than the standard allows is due to certain trends over the years; a moderate-sized Golden is more suitable for the various jobs it performs and will be subject to fewer soundness problems.

Head

Broad in skull, slightly arches laterally and longitudinally without prominence of frontal bones (forehead) or occipital bones. Stop well defined but not abrupt. Foreface deep and wide, nearly as long as skull. Muzzle straight in profile, blending smoothly and strongly into skull; when viewed in profile or from above, slightly deeper and wider at stop than at tip. No heaviness in flews. Removal of whiskers is permitted but not preferred.

Adult male Golden Retrievers are usually 23 to 24 inches tall, with females coming in at about 1½ to 2 inches shorter.

The way the head is proportioned and the facial expressions define the Golden Retriever. The stop is the area between the eyes from the top of the head to the beginning of the muzzle (nose). There should be a definite difference in these two planes. A dog with no stop has only a slope from the head to muzzle as opposed to an angle that indicates depth. The muzzle should taper slightly to the tip of the nose, but it should not be pointed.

Eyes

Friendly and intelligent in expression, medium large with dark, close-fitting

A Golden Retriever's eyes are his most important physical characteristic—they reveal a lot about his personality.

rims, set well apart and reasonably deep in the sockets. Color preferably dark brown, medium brown acceptable, slant eyes and narrow, triangular eyes detract from correct expression and are to be faulted. No white or haw visible when looking straight ahead. Dogs showing evidence of functional abnormality of eyelids or eyelashes (such as, but not limited to, trichiasis, entropian, ectropian or distichiasis) are to be excused from the ring.

HERE'S LOOKING AT YOU

The eyes are the single most important physical characteristic of the Golden. The eyes mirror the dog's personality and character, which are what make a Golden what she is—intelligent, trusting and fun-loving. The eye abnormalities mentioned above need to be diagnosed by a veterinarian.

Teeth

Scissors bite, in which the outer side of the lower incisors touches the inner side of the upper incisors. Undershot or overshot is a disqualification. Misalignment of teeth (irregular placement of incisors) or a level bite (incisors meet each other edge to edge) is undesirable, but not to be confused with overshot or undershot. Full dentition. Obvious gaps are serious faults.

The undershot dog's teeth on the lower jaw protrude beyond her upper-jaw teeth. In the overshot jaw, the upper teeth jut significantly beyond the lower teeth. Another common mouth problem is the wry bite, where the teeth of the upper and lower jaws are offset and do not meet normally when upper and lower teeth meet. Premolars are the teeth usually missing in Goldens, though sometimes molars are, too.

Nose

Black or brownish black, though fading to lighter shade in cold weather not serious. Pink nose or one seriously lacking in pigmentation to be faulted.

Ears

Rather short with front edge attached well behind and just above the eye and falling close to the cheek. When pulled forward, tips of ears should just cover the eyes. Low, hound-like ear set to be faulted.

Correctly sized and placed ears are an important component to the overall look of the Golden.

Neck

Medium long, merging gradually into well laid back shoulders, giving sturdy, muscular appearance. Untrimmed natural ruff. No throatiness.

Body

Well balanced, short coupled, deep through the chest. Chest between forelegs at least as wide as a man's closed hand including thumb, with well developed forechest. Brisket extends to elbow. Ribs long and well sprung but not barrel shaped, extending well towards hindquarters. Loin short, muscular, wide and deep, with very little tuck-up. Back line strong and level from withers to slightly sloping croup, whether standing or moving. Slabsidedness, narrow chest, lack of depth in brisket, sloping backline, roach or sway back, excessive tuck-up, flat or steep croup to be faulted.

FOREQUARTERS
Muscular, well coordinated with hindquarters and capable of free movement.

Whatever your Golden's rating in terms of the breed standard, a healthy puppy with a good personality and temperament will make a wonderful pet.

Shoulder blades long and well laid back with upper tips fairly close together at withers. Upper arms appear about the same length as the blades, setting the elbows back beneath the upper tip of the blades, close to the ribs without looseness. Legs, viewed from the front, straight with good bone, but not to the point of coarseness. Pasterns short and strong, sloping slightly with no suggestion of weakness.

HINDQUARTERS

Broad and strongly muscled. Profile of croup slopes slightly; the pelvic bone slopes at a slightly greater angle (approximately 30 degrees from horizontal). In a natural stance, the femur joins the pelvis at approximately a 90 degree angle; stifles well bent; hocks well let down with short, strong rear pasterns. Legs straight when viewed from rear. Cow hocks, spread hocks and sickle hocks to be faulted.

A SPORTY PHYSIQUE—The description of the manner in which a Golden body should be put together is meant for utilitarian purposes. A sporting dog must have correct structure to perform her job properly. Even if your dog's sole purpose is to be a companion, a correctly structured body will help ensure the active life a Golden relishes. In practical working terms, the strength and power described in the strong neck, broad front, straight legs and correct angles are required for a dog that might spend the day in the field hunting and carrying birds through cover.

Feet

Medium size, round, compact, and well knuckled, with thick pads. Excess hair may be trimmed to show natural size and contour. Dewclaws on forelegs may be removed but are normally left on. Splayed or hare feet to be faulted.

Again, the foot structure described is best for an active, working dog. The faulty hare or splayed foot is one that is pointed in structure as opposed to round. The toes are spread out and the foot itself looks flattened (splayed). Feet like these do not stand up to exercise, and the dog's entire body will eventually suffer.

Tail

Well set on, thick and muscular at the base, following the natural line of the croup. Tail bones extend to, but not below, the point of hock. Carried with

A Golden's over-all appearance should suggest a sturdy, sporty physique.

merry action, level or with moderate upward curve; never curled over back or between legs.

Coat

Dense and water repellent with good undercoat. Outer coat firm and resilient, neither coarse nor silky, lying close to the body; may be straight or wavy. Moderate feathering on back of forelegs and on under-body; heavier feathering on front of neck, back of thighs and underside of tail. Coat on head, paws, and front of legs is short and even. Excessive length, open coats and limp, soft coats are very undesirable. Feet may be trimmed and stray hairs neatened, but the natural appearance of coat or outline should not be altered by cutting or clipping.

The correct Golden coat as described by the standard is necessary for a hunting dog that is used on land and water. The coat should act as a protection to the rough cover that a dog might encounter. A coat of moderate length is desirable, but excessively heavy coats with long feathers are useless for a working dog. The coat should act as a repellent to water, rather than soaking it up like a sponge. A Golden with a proper coat will come out of the water, shake a couple of times and be nearly dry.

Color

Rich, lustrous golden of various shades. Feathering may be lighter than the rest of the body. With exception of graying or lightening of face or body due to age, any white marking, other than a few white hairs on the chest, should be penalized according to its extent. Allowable light shadings are not to be confused with white markings. Predominant body color which is either extremely pale or extremely dark is undesirable. Some latitude should be given to the light puppy whose coloring shows promise of deepening with maturity. Any noticeable area of black or other off-color is a serious fault.

HOW GOLDEN IS GOLDEN?

No other feature of the Golden receives more comment than color. A wide range of colors is permissible, from light to dark golden. It is really a personal preference. The presence of white markings on the body is the fault most easily noticed by the novice.

A light coat like this puppy's will in no way affect her ability to be a good pet.

Gait

When trotting, gait is free, smooth, powerful and well coordinated, showing good reach. Viewed from any position, legs turn neither in nor out, nor do feet cross or interfere with each other. As speed increases, feet tend to converge toward line of balance. It is recommended that dogs be shown on a loose lead to reflect true gait.

This describes the correct movement of a properly structured dog. If a dog moves poorly or inefficiently she will tire more easily. The description above is how dogs are viewed in the showring.

Temperament

Friendly, reliable and trustworthy. Quarrelsomeness or hostility toward other dogs or people in normal situations, or an unwarranted show of timidity or nervousness, is not in keeping with Golden Retriever character. Such actions should be penalized according to their significance.

In the breed ring a judge has very little time to assess a dog's personality. A Golden owner reading this standard has a better knowledge of his or her dog's temperament, though he or she may not be certain of how his or her dog will react to other dogs in stressful environments. A Golden with a good temperament is stable and reacts predictably in any normal situation.

A Golden has a free and smooth gait.

Faults

Any departure from the described ideal should be considered faulty to the degree it interferes with the breed's purpose or is contrary to breed character.

Disqualifications

1. *Deviation in height of more than 1 inch from standard either way.*
2. *Undershot or overshot bite.*

There is no perfect Golden in the world; every dog has some fault or weakness. It is the *overall* appearance and attitude that are most important in evaluating the Golden. There are many faults and a few disqualifications in the Golden Retriever standard, and while they might affect a dog if she were to be entered in a dog show, they will have no bearing on a dog's ability to be a good companion. Remember this when reading the standard and when applying it to your own dog.

CHAPTER SEVEN

A Matter of Fact

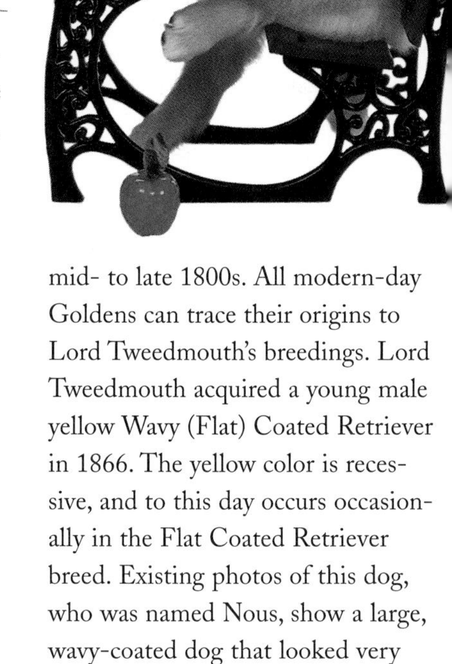

ANCESTRY

Retrievers became increasingly popular in Britain in the 1800s with the growth of the sport of bird hunting. Retrievers were considered the elite of the sporting breeds, as they were so versatile and could be used for waterfowl and upland game. There were many crosses of breeds used during this time, and there is no doubt that several retrievers very Golden-like in appearance existed prior to the actual development of the Golden as we know him today.

It is Sir Dudley Majoribanks, later Lord Tweedmouth, who is credited with the actual creation of the Golden Retriever due to his breeding program in Scotland in the mid- to late 1800s. All modern-day Goldens can trace their origins to Lord Tweedmouth's breedings. Lord Tweedmouth acquired a young male yellow Wavy (Flat) Coated Retriever in 1866. The yellow color is recessive, and to this day occurs occasionally in the Flat Coated Retriever breed. Existing photos of this dog, who was named Nous, show a large, wavy-coated dog that looked very much like a Golden Retriever.

Also acquired was a Tweed Water Spaniel bitch named Belle, a member of another popular hunting breed of the region. These dogs were known for their swimming ability, superior intelligence and wonderful temperaments. They were medium in size, liver colored (any shade of yellow to brown) and had a tightly curled coat with very little feathering.

When one considers that all retriever breeds share a similar genetic base, and that the major difference in the Golden's development from the others is the Tweed Water Spaniel, it is understandable how some of the traits that make the Golden unique from other retriever breeds are derived.

Early Breeding

In England, the first Goldens were registered by the Kennel Club in 1904 and were listed along with Wavy or Flat Coats. After 1913 they were separated by color and known as Golden or Yellow Retrievers. The official term, "Golden Retriever," was not recognized until 1920. Goldens made their first appearance in field trials in the early 1900s and achieved some success. At the same time they began to be entered in dog shows.

One of the most important early breeders was Lord Harcourt, who used the Culham prefix on his dogs. His foundation pair, Culham Brass and Culham Rossa, were descendants of Lord Tweedmouth's Goldens. A grandson of these two, Champion (Ch.) Noranby Campfire, born in 1913, was the first dog to finish a bench championship. Mrs. Charlesworth owned this dog and was a driving force in the breed until the 1950s. Her dogs

The Golden Retriever's ancestry includes a long history as a hunting dog and therefore makes him great outdoor company.

were all registered with the Noranby kennel name.

The two world wars were a serious deterrent to the growth of the breed. During these times breeding almost came to a halt, and dog activities ceased. During World War II some breeders sent their dogs to the United States for safety. After both wars there was a serious drop in quality, as nearly anything that looked like a Golden Retriever was bred to supply demand. An interest in lighter-colored dogs began in the 1930s. Prior to this, most Goldens were relatively dark in color. Eventually the breed standard was changed to allow for light- or cream-colored dogs. This would have an eventual impact on how Goldens would look worldwide.

The term "Golden Retriever" was not officially used until 1920.

Getting to the USA

There are reports of Goldens throughout Canada and the United States in the early 1900s, but none of them were ever registered.

The breed would not make an official entry into the United States until the 1920s. This was an era when Americans were enamored of anything British, including their sporting dogs. Along with Labrador Retrievers, a few Goldens were imported by some of America's wealthiest and most prominent citizens.

Robert Appleton, a resident of East Hampton, Long Island, was the first to actually register a Golden Retriever with the American Kennel Club in 1925. This was an imported 3-year-old male named Lomberdale Blondin. He also imported and registered a female, Dan Hill Judy. These two produced the first registered litter in December 1925.

A Golden's sporting instincts make him eager for anything from duck hunts to backyard games.

During these early years Goldens were registered and shown along with Labrador Retrievers. They did not gain recognition as a separate breed until 1932. During this time, as the handful of fanciers grew, some dogs were shown sporadically, and there was an occasional litter of puppies. However, none of these dogs would go on to have any influence on the breed as it grew. The first truly serious Golden breeder in the United States was Dr. Charles Large of New York City. Beginning in 1931 he imported a number of dogs that were shown and became the basis of his breeding program. He used the kennel name Fernova and was an early activist in the attempt to form a national breed club. His efforts were never realized, because he died in 1933. Most of his dogs were acquired by Michael Clemens, who continued Dr. Large's breedings using the kennel name Frantelle for his dogs.

Goldens of this era that found their way to the estates of the wealthy were acquired not only out of curiosity but also for use as hunting dogs. Few actually made it into homes or lived as pets. They were usually in large kennel facilities overseen by the kennel managers. It is interesting to note that a Golden was entered in the first AKC

WHERE DID DOGS COME FROM?

It can be argued that dogs were right there at man's side from the beginning of time. As soon as human beings began to document their existence, the dog was among their drawings and inscriptions. Dogs were not just friends, they served a purpose: There were dogs to hunt birds, pull sleds, herd sheep, burrow after rats—even sit in laps! What your dog was originally bred to do influences the way he behaves. The American Kennel Club recognizes over 140 breeds, and there are hundreds more distinct breeds around the world. To make sense of the breeds, they are grouped according to their size or function. The AKC has seven groups:

1. Sporting
2. Working
3. Herding
4. Hounds
5. Terriers
6. Toys
7. Nonsporting

Can you name a breed from each group? Here's some help: (1) Golden Retriever, (2) Doberman Pinscher, (3) Collie, (4) Beagle, (5) Scottish Terrier, (6) Maltese and (7) Dalmatian. All modern domestic dogs (*Canis familiaris*) are related, however different they look, and are all descended from *Canis lupus*, the gray wolf.

Licensed Retriever Field Trial held on Long Island in 1931. This young imported female went on to become Ch. Lady Burns and was one of two entered in the Puppy Stake.

The Golden Retriever finally received the boost he needed when Col. Samuel Magoffin of Vancouver, British Columbia, imported a young male from England named Speedwell Pluto in 1932. Pluto was a champion in both the United States and Canada. He was the first Golden to win a Best in Show Award and was a successful hunting dog as well. He is considered to be the foundation sire of the breed in America. Col. Magoffin's Rockhaven Kennels were based in Vancouver. He also founded Gilnockie Kennels, located in Englewood, Colorado. He imported a number of dogs from England that would be influential in the development of the Golden breed.

MIDWESTERN GOLDENS

Another early Golden fancier in Minnesota was Henry Christian, who started Goldwood Kennels in 1933. He imported Sprite of Aldgrove from England and a Ch. Speedwell Pluto son, Rockhaven Rory, from Canada. Both would complete their championships. Rory was one of the most widely used stud dogs among breeders in the area. Goldwood Kennels produced FC Goldwood Tuck and two of the first great Golden obedience competitors, Goldwood Michael UD and Goldwood Toby UD. The latter was the first Golden to earn a Utility Degree.

The St. Louis, Missouri, area was another region of early Golden activity. Mr. and Mrs. Mahlon Wallace, Jr., and John K. Wallace began importing from England in 1933. The breeding of two of their imports, Speedwell Reuben and Ch. Speedwell Tango, resulted in FC Rip. In 1939 he was the first Golden to complete a field championship.

Another early English import whose influence must be mentioned is Eng. Ch. Marine of Woolley. He was imported and owned by Blue Leader Kennels of Santa Barbara, California, and was one of the first Goldens in that section of the country. Marine is important as he sired littermates Rockhaven Ben Bolt and Rockhaven Judy, both imported to Minnesota from Canada. Ben Bolt was owned by Ralph Boalt, was run in field trials and was an influential sire of the breed in the late 1930s and 1940s in the area. Judy was one of the foundation dams of Woodend Kennels. She produced several top field dogs that would become important as the Golden gained popularity as a field competitor.

Goldens are eager to work and too energetic to remain happy when penned up for long periods of time.

The growth and popularity of the Golden in the Midwest in these years were a remarkable phenomenon. This was an era when hunting upland game and waterfowl was enjoying its peak in popularity among a growing number of hunters, and the Midwest was the capital of this pastime. The Golden was embraced by many hunters as the dog for the job. Through the mid-1940s half of the Golden litters

The GRCA's members breed Goldens that are exceptional examples of the breed.

registered by the American Kennel Club were whelped in southeastern Minnesota.

American breeders continued to import Goldens from England, and while most had little or no impact on the breed as a whole, in the late 1960s several imports began to make a difference. The greatest change was that coats of lighter color were seen more frequently. Gradually the lighter color became increasingly popular with show fanciers and eventually with the public seeking Goldens. The dogs now imported from England were not only different in color but also in overall type than the darker American Golden that had been developed from English stock of a different era.

Forming the GRCA

It was through the impetus of the midwestern fanciers that the Golden Retriever Club of America (GRCA) was formed in 1939. Its first president was John K. Wallace. The Club is the guiding force in ensuring that the breed standard, character and original purpose are upheld. The GRCA encourages its members only to breed Goldens that are not only good physical representatives of the breed but are also genetically sound and possess true Golden personalities.

Striking Gold in Obedience

It was in the 1970s that Goldens emerged as one of the premier dogs for obedience competition. When the Obedience Trial Champion title was initiated in July 1977, the first three dogs of any breed to attain it were Golden Retrievers. Since then more Goldens have earned the title than any other breed. Goldens that excel in obedience come from all backgrounds: field, show and pet. The prerequisite is a willing attitude and athletic ability.

As mentioned earlier, Goldens up to this time were not a popular breed. They were a well-kept secret and often confused with Irish Setters. The event that signaled the sudden growth and brought the Golden prominence with the American public was when President Gerald Ford obtained a young Golden female in 1974. Liberty and her subsequent litter of puppies received national publicity. The secret was out. Golden registrations skyrocketed and suddenly the breed was ranked in the top five in popularity, where it continues to hover to this day.

Once primarily sought after for his abilities as a hunting dog, the Golden is now employed in a variety of jobs. They are commonly used by the various organizations that provide sighted guides for the blind, ears for the deaf and service dogs for the handicapped. Many Goldens are well suited to these tasks because of

Famous Owners of Golden Retrievers

Oprah Winfrey	Ed McMahon
Mary Tyler Moore	Bob Newhart
Gerald Ford	Chevy Chase
Jimmy Stewart	Frank Gifford
Bill Blass	

A Golden's instinct to retrieve isn't limited to water-fowl—a rubber ball will work just as well.

Goldens have long since surpassed their value as just sporting dogs—they make the best kind of family pet.

their intelligence, trainability, stability and loyalty. Goldens are also trained and utilized as rescue dogs in numerous situations, such as earthquake relief, avalanches or seeking lost persons. Their natural scenting abilities, along with the power to concentrate on the task at hand, make them popular dogs for such work. There is rarely a day that goes by when a Golden isn't seen in a television or magazine ad. They are easy to work with and their expressive faces are good subjects for the media.

CHAPTER EIGHT

On Good Behavior

by Ian Dunbar, Ph.D., MRCVS

Training is the jewel in the crown—the most important aspect of doggy husbandry. There is no more important variable influencing dog behavior and temperament than the dog's education: A well-trained, well-behaved and good-natured puppydog is always a joy to live with, but an untrained and uncivilized dog can be a perpetual nightmare. Moreover, deny the dog an education and she will not have the opportunity to fulfill her own canine potential; neither will she have the ability to communicate effectively with her human companions.

Luckily, modern psychological training methods are easy, efficient, effective and, above all, considerably dog-friendly and user-friendly.

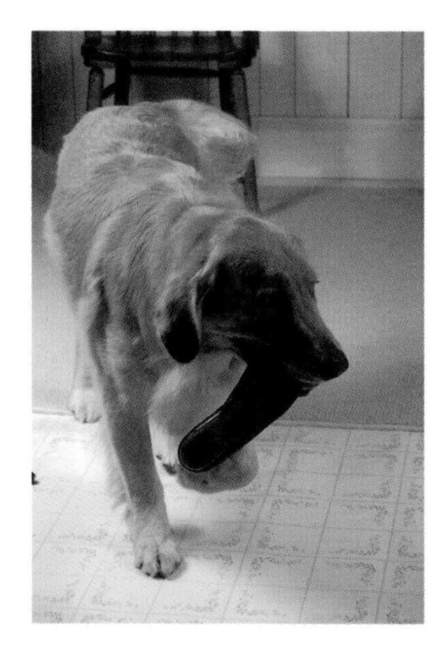

Your Golden may try to help around the house and "retrieve" your shoes unless you teach her not to.

Doggy education is as simple as it is enjoyable. But before you can have a good time play-training with your new dog, you have to learn what to do and how to do it. There is no bigger variable influencing the success of dog training than the owner's experience and expertise. Before you embark on the dog's education, you must first educate yourself.

Basic Training for Owners

Ideally, basic owner training should begin well before you select your dog. Find out all you can about your chosen breed first, then master rudimentary training and handling skills. If you already have your puppydog, owner training is a dire emergency—the clock is ticking! Especially for puppies, the first few weeks at home are the most important and influential days in the dog's life. Indeed, the cause of most adolescent and adult problems may be traced back to the initial days the pup explores her new home. This is the time to establish the *status quo*—to teach the puppydog how you would like her to behave and so prevent otherwise quite predictable problems.

In addition to consulting breeders and breed books, seek out as many pet owners with your breed as you can find. Find out the breed-specific problems, so you can nip them in the bud. In particular, you should talk to owners with adolescent dogs and make a list of all anticipated problems. Most important, test drive at least half a dozen adolescent and adult dogs of your breed yourself. An 8-week-old puppy is deceptively easy to handle, but she will acquire adult size, speed and strength in just four months, so you should learn now what to prepare for.

Puppy and pet dog training classes offer a convenient venue to locate pet owners and observe dogs in action. For a list of suitable trainers in your area, contact the Association of Pet Dog Trainers at 800-PET-DOGS.

Principles of Training

Most people think training comprises teaching the dog to do things such as sit, speak and roll over, but even a 4-week-old pup knows how to do these things already. Instead, the first step in training involves teaching the dog human words for each dog behavior and activity and for each aspect of the dog's environment. That way you, the owner, can more easily participate in the dog's domestic education by directing her to perform specific actions appropriately, that is, at the right time, in the right place and so on. Training opens communication channels, enabling an educated dog to at least understand her owner's requests.

In addition to teaching a dog what we want her to do, it is also necessary to teach her why she should do what we ask. Indeed, 95 percent of training revolves around motivating the dog to want to do what we want. Dogs often understand what their owners want; they just don't see the point of doing it—especially when the owner's repetitively boring and seemingly senseless instructions are totally at odds with much more pressing and exciting doggy distractions. It is not so much the dog that is being stubborn or dominant; rather, it is the owner who has failed to acknowledge the dog's needs and feelings and to approach training from the dog's point of view.

The Meaning of Instructions

The secret to successful training is learning how to use training lures to predict or prompt specific behaviors—to coax the dog to do what you want when you want. Any highly valued object (such as a treat or toy) may be used as a lure, which the dog will follow with her eyes and nose. Moving the lure in specific ways entices the dog to move her nose, head and entire body in specific ways. In fact, by learning the art of manipulating various lures, it is possible to teach the dog to assume virtually any body position and perform any action. Once you have control over the expression of the dog's behaviors and can elicit any body position or behavior at will, you can easily teach the dog to perform on request.

Tell your dog what you want her to do, use a lure to entice her to respond correctly, then profusely praise and maybe reward her once she performs the desired action. For example, verbally request "Fido, sit!" while you move a squeaky toy upwards and backwards over the dog's muzzle (lure-movement and hand signal), smile knowingly as she looks up (to follow the lure) and sits down (as a result of canine anatomical engineering), then praise her to distraction ("Gooood Fido!"). Squeak the toy, offer a training treat and give your dog and yourself a pat on the back.

Being able to elicit desired responses over and over enables the owner to reward the dog over and over. Consequently, the dog begins to think training is fun. For example, the more the dog is rewarded for sitting, the more she enjoys sitting. Eventually the dog comes to realize that, whereas most sitting is appreciated, sitting immediately upon request usually prompts especially enthusiastic praise and a slew of high-level rewards. The dog begins to sit on cue much of the time, showing that she is starting to grasp the meaning of the owner's verbal request and hand signal.

Why Comply?

Most dogs enjoy initial lure-reward training and are only too happy to comply with their owners' wishes. Unfortunately, repetitive drilling without appreciative feedback tends to diminish the dog's enthusiasm until she eventually fails to see the point of complying anymore. Moreover, as the dog approaches adolescence she becomes more easily distracted as she develops other interests. Lengthy sessions with repetitive exercises tend to bore and demotivate both parties. If it's not fun, the owner doesn't do it and neither does the dog. Integrate training into your dog's life: The greater the number of training sessions each day and the shorter they are, the more willingly compliant your dog will become.

Punishment

Without a doubt, lure-reward training is by far the best way to teach: Entice your dog to do what you want and then reward her for doing so. Unfortunately, a human shortcoming is to take the good for granted and to moan and groan at the bad. Specifically, the dog's many good behaviors are ignored while the owner focuses on punishing the dog for making mistakes. In extreme cases, instruction is limited to punishing mistakes made by a trainee dog, child, employee or husband, even though it has been proven punishment training is notoriously inefficient and ineffective and is decidedly unfriendly and combative. It teaches the dog that training is a drag, almost as quickly as it teaches the dog to dislike her trainer. Why treat our best friends like our worst enemies?

Punishment training is also much more laborious and time consuming. Whereas it takes only a finite amount of time to teach a dog what to chew, for example, it takes much, much longer to punish the dog for each and every mistake. Remember, there is only one right way! So why not teach that right way from the outset?!

To make matters worse, punishment training causes severe lapses in the dog's reliability. Since it is obviously impossible to punish the dog each and every time she misbehaves, the dog quickly learns to distinguish between those times when she must comply (so as to avoid impending punishment) and those times when she need not comply, because punishment is impossible. Such times include when the dog is off leash and 6 feet away, when the owner is otherwise engaged (talking to a friend, watching television, taking a shower, tending to the baby or chatting on the telephone) or when the dog is left at home alone.

Instances of misbehavior will be numerous when the owner is away, because even when the dog complied in the owner's looming presence, she did so unwillingly. The dog was forced to act against her will, rather than molding her will to want to please. Hence, when the owner is absent, not only does the dog know she need not comply, she simply does not want to. Again, the trainee is not a stubborn vindictive beast, but rather the trainer has failed to teach. Punishment training invariably creates unpredictable Jekyll and Hyde behavior.

Trainer's Tools

Many training books extol the virtues of a vast array of training paraphernalia. In reality, most effective training tools are not found in stores; they come from within ourselves. In addition to a willing dog, all you really need is a functional human brain, gentle hands, a loving heart and a good attitude.

In terms of equipment, all dogs do require a quality buckle collar to sport dog tags and to attach the leash (for safety and to comply with local leash laws). Hollow chew toys (like Kongs or sterilized longbones) and a dog bed or collapsible crate are musts for housetraining. Three additional tools are required for training:

1. specific lures (training treats and toys) to predict and prompt specific desired behaviors;

2. rewards (praise, affection, training treats and toys) to reinforce for the dog what a lot of fun it all is; and

3. knowledge—how to convert the dog's favorite activities and games (potential distractions to training) into "life-rewards," which may be employed to facilitate training.

The most powerful of these is knowledge. Education is the key!

Housetraining

If dogs were left to their own devices, certainly they would chew, dig and bark for entertainment and then no doubt highlight a few areas of their living space with sprinkles of urine, in much the same way we decorate by hanging pictures. Consequently, when we ask a dog to live with us, we must teach her *where* she may dig, *where* she may perform her toilet duties, *what* she may chew and *when* she may bark. After all, when left at home alone for many hours, we cannot expect the dog to amuse herself by completing crosswords or watching the soaps on TV!

Also, it would be decidedly unfair to keep the house rules a secret from the dog, and then get angry and punish the poor critter for inevitably transgressing rules she did not even know existed. Remember: Without adequate education and guidance, the dog will be forced to establish her own rules—doggy rules—and most probably will be at odds with the owner's view of domestic living.

Since most problems develop during the first few days the dog is at home, prospective dog owners must be certain they are quite clear about the principles of housetraining *before* they get a dog. Early misbehaviors quickly become established as the *status quo*—becoming firmly entrenched as hard-to-break bad habits, which set the precedent for years to come. Make sure to teach your dog good habits right from the start. Good habits are just as hard to break as bad ones!

Ideally, when a new dog comes home, try to arrange for someone to be present as much as possible during the first few days (for adult dogs) or weeks for puppies. With only a little forethought, it is surprisingly easy to find a puppy sitter, such as a retired person, who would be willing to eat from your refrigerator and watch your television while keeping an eye on the newcomer to encourage the dog to play with chew toys and to ensure she goes outside on a regular basis.

Potty Training

To teach the dog where to relieve herself:

1. never let her make a single mistake;
2. let her know where you want her to go; and
3. handsomely reward her for doing so: "GOOOOOOOD DOG!!!" liver treat, liver treat, liver treat!

Preventing Mistakes

A single mistake is a training disaster, since it heralds many more in future weeks. And each time the dog soils the house, this further reinforces the dog's unfortunate preference for an indoor, carpeted toilet. Do not let an unhousetrained dog have full run of the house.

When you are away from home, or cannot pay full attention, confine the dog to an area where elimination is appropriate, such as an outdoor run or, better still, a small, comfortable indoor kennel with access to an outdoor run. When confined in this manner, most dogs will naturally housetrain themselves.

If that's not possible, confine the dog to an area, such as a utility room, kitchen, basement or garage, where elimination may not be desired in the long run but as an interim measure it is certainly preferable to doing it all around the house. Use newspaper to cover the floor of the dog's day room. The newspaper may be used to soak up the urine and to wrap up and dispose of the feces. Once your dog develops a preferred spot for eliminating, it is only necessary to cover that part of the floor with newspaper. The smaller papered area may then be moved (only a little each day) towards the door to the outside. Thus the dog will develop the tendency to go to the door when she needs to relieve herself.

Never confine an unhousetrained dog to a crate for long periods. Doing so would force the dog to soil the crate and ruin its usefulness as an aid for housetraining (see the following discussion).

Teaching Where

In order to teach your dog where you would like her to do her business, you have to be there to direct the proceedings—an obvious, yet often neglected, fact of life. In order to be there to teach the dog where to go, you need to know *when* she needs to go. Indeed, the success of housetraining depends on the owner's ability to predict these times. Certainly, a regular feeding schedule will facilitate prediction somewhat, but there is nothing like "loading the deck" and influencing the timing of the outcome yourself!

Whenever you are at home, make sure the dog is under constant supervision and/or confined to a small area. If already well trained, simply instruct the dog to lie down in her bed or basket. Alternatively, confine the dog to a crate (doggy den) or tie-down (a short, 18-inch lead that can be clipped to an eye hook in the baseboard near her bed). Short-term close confinement strongly inhibits urination and defecation, since the dog does not want to soil her sleeping area. Thus, when you release the puppydog each hour, she will definitely need to urinate immediately and defecate every third or fourth hour. Keep the dog confined to her doggy den and take her to her intended toilet area each hour, every hour and on the hour.

When taking your dog outside, instruct her to sit quietly before opening the door—she will soon learn to sit by the door when she needs to go out!

Teaching Why

Being able to predict when the dog needs to go enables the owner to be on the spot to praise and reward the dog. Each hour, hurry the dog to the intended toilet area in the yard, issue the appropriate instruction ("Go pee!" or "Go poop!"), then give the dog three to four minutes to produce. Praise and offer a couple of training treats when successful. The treats are important because many people fail to praise their dogs with feeling . . . and housetraining is hardly the time for understatement. So either loosen up and enthusiastically praise that dog: "Wuzzzer-wuzzer-wuzzer, hoooser good wuffer den? Hoooo went pee for Daddy?" Or say "Good dog!" as best you can and offer the treats for effect.

Following elimination is an ideal time for a spot of play-training in the yard or house. Also, an empty dog may be allowed greater freedom around the house for the next half hour or so, just as long as you keep an eye out to make sure she does not get into other kinds of mischief. If you are preoccupied and cannot pay full attention, confine the dog to her doggy den once more to enjoy a peaceful snooze or to play with her many chew toys.

If your dog does not eliminate within the allotted time outside—no biggie! Back to her doggy den, and then try again after another hour.

Beware of falling into the trap of walking the dog to get her to eliminate. The good ol' dog walk is such an enormous highlight in the dog's life that it represents the single biggest potential reward in domestic dogdom. However, when in a hurry, or during inclement weather, many owners abruptly terminate the walk the moment the dog has done her business. This, in effect, severely punishes the dog for doing the right thing, in the right place at the right time. Consequently, many dogs become strongly inhibited from eliminating outdoors because they know it will signal an abrupt end to an otherwise thoroughly enjoyable walk.

Instead, instruct the dog to relieve herself in the yard prior to going for a walk. You will find with a "No feces—no walk" policy, your dog will become one of the fastest defecators in the business.

If you do not have a backyard, instruct the dog to eliminate right outside your front door prior to the walk. Not only will this facilitate clean up and disposal of the feces in your own trash can but, also, the walk may again be used as a colossal reward.

Chewing and Barking

Short-term close confinement also teaches the dog that occasional quiet moments are a reality of domestic living. Your puppydog is extremely impressionable during her first few weeks at home. Regular confinement at this time soon exerts a calming influence over the dog's personality. Remember, once the dog is housetrained and calmer, there will be a whole lifetime ahead for the dog to enjoy full run of the house and garden. On the other hand, by letting the newcomer have unrestricted access to the entire household and allowing her to run willy-nilly, she will most certainly develop a bunch of behavior problems in short order, no doubt necessitating confinement later in life.

When confining the dog, make sure she always has an impressive array of suitable chew toys. Kongs and sterilized longbones (both readily available from pet stores) make the best chew toys, since they are hollow and may be stuffed with treats to heighten the dog's interest.

Remember, treats do not have to be junk food and they certainly should not represent extra calories. Rather, treats should be part of each dog's regular daily diet: Some food may be served in the dog's bowl for breakfast and dinner, some food may be used as training treats, and some food may be used for stuffing chew toys. I regularly stuff my dogs' many Kongs with different shaped biscuits and kibble. The kibble seems to fall out fairly easily, as do the oval-shaped biscuits, thus rewarding the dog instantaneously for checking out the chew toys. The bone-shaped biscuits fall out after a while, rewarding the dog for worrying at the chew toy. But the triangular biscuits never come out. They remain inside the Kong as lures, maintaining the dog's fascination with her chew toy. To further focus the dog's interest, I always make sure to flavor the triangular biscuits by rubbing them with a little cheese or freeze-dried liver.

If stuffed chew toys are reserved especially for times the dog is confined, the puppydog will soon learn to enjoy quiet moments in her doggy den and she will quickly develop a chew-toy habit—a good habit! This is a simple autoshaping process; all the owner has to do is set up the situation and the dog all but trains herself—easy and effective. Even when the dog is given run of the house, her first inclination will be to indulge her rewarding chew-toy habit rather than destroy less attractive household articles, such as curtains, carpets, chairs and compact disks. Similarly, a chew-toy chewer will be less inclined to scratch and chew herself excessively. Also, if the dog busies herself as a recreational chewer, she will be less inclined to develop into a recreational barker or digger when left at home alone.

Stuff a number of chew toys whenever the dog is left confined and remove the extra-special-tasting treats when you return. Your dog will now amuse herself with her chew toys before falling asleep and then resume playing with her chew toys when she expects you to return. Since most owner-absent misbehavior happens right after you leave and right before your expected return, your puppydog will now be conveniently preoccupied with her chew toys at these times.

Come and Sit

Most puppies will happily approach virtually anyone, whether called or not; that is, until they collide with adolescence and develop other more important doggy interests, such as sniffing different odors on the grass. Your mission, Mr./Ms. Owner, is to teach and reward the pup for coming reliably, willingly and happily when called—and you have just three months to get it done. Unless adequately reinforced, your puppy's tendency to approach people will self-destruct by adolescence.

Call your dog ("Fido, come!"), open your arms (and maybe squat down) as a welcoming signal, waggle a treat or toy as a lure and reward the puppydog when she comes running. Do not wait to praise the dog until she reaches you—she may come 95 percent of the way and then run off after some distraction. Instead, praise the dog's first step towards you and continue praising enthusiastically for every step she takes in your direction.

To teach come, call your dog, open your arms as a welcoming signal, wave a toy or a treat and praise for every step in your direction.

When the rapidly approaching puppydog is three lengths away from impact, instruct her to sit ("Fido, sit!") and hold the lure in front of you in an outstretched hand to prevent her from hitting you mid-chest and knocking you flat on your back! As Fido decelerates to nose the lure, move the treat upwards and backwards just over her muzzle with an upwards motion of your extended arm (palm-upwards). As the dog looks up to follow the lure, she will sit down (if she jumps up, you are holding the lure too high). Praise the dog for sitting. Move backwards and call her again. Repeat this many times over, always praising when Fido comes and sits; on occasion, reward her.

For the first couple of trials, use a training treat both as a lure to entice the dog to come and sit and as a reward for doing so. Thereafter, try to use different items as lures and rewards. After just a few repetitions, dispense with the lures and rewards; the dog will begin to respond willingly to your verbal requests and hand signals just for the prospect of praise from your heart and affection from your hands.

Instruct every family member, friend and visitor how to get the dog to come and sit. Unless you teach your dog how to meet people, that is, to sit for greetings, no doubt the dog will resort to jumping up. Then you and the visitors will get annoyed, and the dog will be punished. This is not fair.

Even though your dog quickly masters obedient recalls in the house, her reliability may falter when playing in the backyard or local park. Ironically, it is the owner who has unintentionally trained the dog not to respond in these instances. By allowing the dog to play and run around and otherwise have a good time, but then calling the dog to put her on leash to take her home, the dog quickly learns playing is fun but training is a drag. Thus, playing in the park becomes a severe distraction, which works against training. Bad news!

Instead, whether playing with the dog off leash or on leash, request her to come at frequent intervals—say, every minute or so. On most occasions, praise and pet the dog for a few seconds while she is sitting, then tell her to go play again. For especially fast recalls, offer a couple of training treats and take the time to praise and pet the dog enthusiastically before releasing her. The dog will learn that coming when called is not necessarily the end of the play session; rather, it signals an enjoyable, quality time-out with the owner before resuming play once more. In fact, playing in the park now becomes a very effective life-reward, which works to facilitate training by reinforcing each obedient and timely recall. Good news!

Sit, Down, Stand and Rollover

Teaching the dog a variety of body positions is easy for owner and dog, impressive for spectators and extremely useful for all. Using lure-reward techniques, it is possible to train several positions at once to verbal commands or hand signals (which impress the socks off onlookers).

Sit and down—the two control commands—prevent or resolve nearly a hundred behavior problems. For example, if the dog happily and obediently sits or lies down when requested, she cannot jump on visitors, dash out the front door, pester other dogs, harass cats or annoy family, friends or strangers. Additionally, "Sit" or "Down" are the best emergency commands for off-leash control.

It is easier to teach and maintain a reliable sit than maintain a reliable recall. Sit is the purest and simplest of commands—either the dog is sitting or she is not. If there is any change of circumstances or potential danger in the park, for example, simply instruct the dog to sit. If she sits, you have a number of options: Allow the dog to resume playing when she is safe, walk up and put the dog on leash or call the dog. The dog will be much more likely to come when called if she has already acknowledged her compliance by sitting. If the dog does not sit in the park—train her to!

Stand and rollover-stay are the two positions for examining the dog. Your veterinarian will love you to distraction if you take a little time to teach the dog to stand still and roll over and play possum.

As with teaching come and sit, the training techniques to teach the dog to assume all other body positions on cue are user-friendly and dog-friendly. Simply give the appropriate request, lure the dog into the desired body position using a training treat or toy and then praise (and maybe reward) the dog as soon as she complies. Try not to touch the dog to get her to respond. If you teach the dog by guiding her into position, the dog will quickly learn that rump-pressure means sit, for example, but as yet you still have no control over your dog if she is just 6 feet away. It will still be necessary to teach the dog to sit on request. So do not make training a time-consuming two-step process; instead, teach the dog to sit to a verbal request or hand signal from the outset. Once the dog sits willingly when requested, by all means use your hands to pet the dog when she does so.

To teach down when the dog is already sitting, say "Fido, down!," hold the lure in one hand (palm down) and lower that hand to the floor between the dog's forepaws. As the dog lowers her head to follow the lure, slowly move the lure away from the dog just a fraction (in front of her paws). The dog will lie down as she stretches her nose forward to follow the lure. Praise the dog when she does so. If the dog stands up, you pulled the lure away too far and too quickly.

When teaching the dog to lie down from the standing position, say "Down" and lower the lure to the floor as before. Once the dog has lowered her forequarters and assumed a play bow, gently and slowly move the lure towards the dog between her forelegs. Praise the dog as soon as her rear end plops down.

You will notice the more energetically you move your arm—upwards (palm up) to get the dog to sit, and downwards (palm down) to get the dog to lie down—the more energetically the dog responds to your requests. Now try training the dog in silence and you will notice she has also learned to respond to hand signals. Yeah! Not too shabby for the first session.

To teach stand from the sitting position, say "Fido, stand," slowly move the lure half a dog-length away from the dog's nose, keeping it at nose level, and praise the dog as she stands to follow the lure. As soon as the dog stands, lower the lure to just beneath the dog's chin to entice her to look down; otherwise she will stand and then sit immediately. To prompt the dog to stand from the down position, move the lure half a dog-length upwards and away from the dog, holding the lure at standing nose height from the floor.

Teaching rollover is best started from the down position, with the dog lying on one side, or at least with both hind legs stretched out on the same side. Say "Fido, bang!" and move the lure backwards and alongside the dog's muzzle to her elbow (on the side of her outstretched hind legs). Once the dog looks to the side and backwards, very slowly move the lure upwards to the dog's shoulder and backbone. Tickling the dog in the goolies (groin area) often invokes a reflex-raising of the hind leg as an appeasement gesture, which facilitates the tendency to roll over. If you move the lure too quickly and the dog jumps into the standing position, have patience and start again. As soon as the dog rolls onto her back, keep the lure stationary and mesmerize the dog with a relaxing tummy rub.

To teach rollover-stay when the dog is standing or moving, say "Fido, bang!" and give the appropriate hand signal (with index finger pointed and thumb cocked in true Sam Spade fashion), then in one fluid movement lure her to first lie down and then rollover-stay as above.

Teaching the dog to stay in each of the above four positions becomes a piece of cake after first teaching the dog not to worry at the toy or treat training lure. This is best accomplished by hand feeding dinner kibble. Hold a piece of kibble firmly in your hand and softly instruct "Off!" Ignore any licking and slobbering for however long the dog worries at the treat, but say "Take it!" and offer the kibble *the*

Using a food lure to teach sit, down and stand. 1) "Phoenix, sit." 2) Hand palm upwards, move lure up and back over dog's muzzle. 3) "Good sit, Phoenix!"

4) "Phoenix, down." 5) Hand palm downwards, move lure down to lie between dog's forepaws. 6) "Phoenix, off. Good down, Phoenix!"

7) "Phoenix, sit!" 8) Palm upwards, move lure up and back, keeping it close to dog's muzzle. 9) "Good sit, Phoenix!"

10) "Phoenix, stand!"
11) Move lure away from dog at nose height, then lower it a tad.
12) "Phoenix, off! Good stand, Phoenix!"

13) "Phoenix, down!"
14) Hand palm downwards, move lure down to lie between dog's forepaws.
15) "Phoenix, off! Good down-stay, Phoenix!"

16) "Phoenix, stand!"
17) Move lure away from dog's muzzle up to nose height.
18) "Phoenix, off! Good stand-stay, Phoenix. Now we'll make the vet and groomer happy!"

instant the dog breaks contact with her muzzle. Repeat this a few times, and then up the ante and insist the dog remove her muzzle for one whole second before offering the kibble. Then progressively refine your criteria and have the dog not touch your hand (or treat) for longer and longer periods on each trial, such as for two seconds, four seconds, then six, ten, fifteen, twenty, thirty seconds and so on.

The dog soon learns: (1) worrying at the treat never gets results, whereas (2) noncontact is often rewarded after a variable time lapse.

Teaching "Off!" has many useful applications in its own right. Additionally, instructing the dog not to touch a training lure often produces spontaneous and magical stays. Request the dog to stand-stay, for example, and not to touch the lure. At first set your sights on a short two-second stay before rewarding the dog. (Remember, every long journey begins with a single step.) However, on subsequent trials, gradually and progressively increase the length of stay required to receive a reward. In no time at all your dog will stand calmly for a minute or so.

Relevancy Training

Once you have taught the dog what you expect her to do when requested to come, sit, lie down, stand, rollover and stay, the time is right to teach the dog why she should comply with your wishes. The secret is to have many (many) extremely short training interludes (two to five seconds each) at numerous times during the course of the dog's day.

In no time at all the dog will be only too pleased to follow your instructions because she has learned that a compliant response heralds all sorts of goodies. Basically all you are trying to teach the dog is how to say please: "Please throw the tennis ball. Please may I snuggle on the couch."

In fact, the dog may be unable to distinguish between training and good times and, indeed, there should be no distinction. The warped concept that training involves forcing the dog to comply and/or dominating her will is totally at odds with the picture of a truly well-trained dog. In reality, enjoying a game of training with a dog is no different from enjoying a game of backgammon or tennis with a friend; and walking with a dog should be no different from strolling with a spouse, or with buddies on the golf course.

Walk by Your Side

Many people attempt to teach a dog to heel by putting her on a leash and physically correcting the dog when she makes mistakes. There are a number of things seriously wrong with this approach, the first being that most people do not want precision heeling; rather, they simply want the dog to follow or walk by their side. Second, when physically restrained during "training," even though the dog may grudgingly mope by your side when "handcuffed" on leash, let's see what happens when she is off leash. History! The dog is in the next county because she never enjoyed walking with you on leash and you have no control over her off leash. So let's just teach the dog off leash from the outset to want to walk with us. Third, if the dog has not been trained to heel, it is a trifle hasty to think about punishing the poor dog for making mistakes and breaking heeling rules she didn't even know existed. This is simply not fair! Surely, if the dog had been adequately taught how to heel, she would seldom make mistakes and hence there would be no need to correct the dog. Remember, each mistake and each correction (punishment) advertise the trainer's inadequacy, not the dog's. The dog is not stubborn, she is not stupid and she is not bad. Even if she were, she would still require training, so let's train her properly.

Let's teach the dog to enjoy following us and to want to walk by our side off leash. Then it will be easier to teach high-precision off-leash heeling patterns if desired. Before going on outdoor walks, it is necessary to teach the dog not to pull. Then it becomes easy to teach on-leash walking and heeling because the dog already wants to walk with you, she is familiar with the desired walking and heeling positions and she knows not to pull.

Following

Start by training your dog to follow you. Many puppies will follow if you

To get your puppy used to the feel of a leash, put him on it for a few short trips around the house.

simply walk away from them and maybe click your fingers or chuckle. Adult dogs may require additional enticement to stimulate them to follow, such as a training lure or, at the very least, a lively trainer. To teach the dog to follow: (1) keep walking and (2) walk away from the dog. If the dog attempts to lead or lag, change pace; slow down if the dog forges too far ahead, but speed up if she lags too far behind. Say "Steady!" or "Easy!" each time before you slow down and "Quickly!" or "Hustle!" each time before you speed up, and the dog will learn to change pace on cue. If the dog lags or leads too far, or if she wanders right or left, simply walk quickly in the opposite direction and maybe even run away from the dog and hide.

Practicing is a lot of fun; you can set up a course in your home, yard or park to do this. Indoors, entice the dog to follow upstairs, into a bedroom, into the bathroom, downstairs, around the living room couch, zigzagging between dining room chairs and into the kitchen for dinner. Outdoors, get the dog to follow around park benches, trees, shrubs and along walkways and lines in the grass. (For safety outdoors, it is advisable to attach a long line on the dog, but never exert corrective tension on the line.)

Remember, following has a lot to do with attitude—your attitude! Most probably your dog will not want to follow Mr. Grumpy Troll with the personality of wilted lettuce. Lighten up—walk with a jaunty step, whistle a happy tune, sing, skip and tell jokes to your dog and she will be right by your side.

By Your Side

It is smart to train the dog to walk close on one side or the other—either side will do, your choice. When walking, jogging or cycling, it is generally bad news to have the dog suddenly cut in front of you. In fact, I train my dogs to walk "By my side" and "Other side"—both very useful instructions. It is possible to position the dog fairly accurately by looking to the appropriate side and clicking your fingers or slapping your thigh on that side. A precise positioning may be attained by holding a training lure, such as a chew toy, tennis ball or food treat. Stop and stand still several times throughout the walk, just as you would when window shopping or meeting a friend. Use the lure to make sure the dog slows down and stays close whenever you stop.

When teaching the dog to heel, we generally want her to sit in heel position when we stop. Teach heel position at the standstill and the dog will learn that the default heel position is sitting by your side (left or right—your choice, unless you wish to compete in obedience trials, in which case the dog must heel on the left).

Several times a day, stand up and call your dog to come and sit in heel position—"Fido, heel!" For example, instruct the dog to come to heel each time there are commercials on TV, or each time you turn a page of a novel, and the dog will get it in a single evening.

Practice straight-line heeling and turns separately. With the dog sitting at heel, teach her to turn in place. After each quarter-turn, half-turn or full turn in place, lure the dog to sit at heel. Now it's time for short straight-line heeling sequences, no more than a few steps at a time. Always think of heeling in terms of sit-heel-sit sequences—start and end with the dog in position and do your best to keep her there when moving. Progressively increase the number of steps in each sequence. When the dog remains close for 20 yards of

Your dog will quickly learn that the appearance of a leash means the arrival of a long-awaited trip outdoors.

Golden puppies, like all young dogs, will need to have their insatiable energy and curiosity reigned in by efficient training.

straight-line heeling, it is time to add a few turns and then sign up for a happy-heeling obedience class to get some advice from the experts.

No Pulling on Leash

You can start teaching your dog not to pull on leash anywhere—in front of the television or outdoors—but regardless of location, you must not take a single step with tension in the leash. For a reason known only to dogs, even just a couple of paces of pulling on leash is intrinsically motivating and diabolically rewarding. Instead, attach the leash to the dog's collar, grasp the other end firmly with both hands held close to your chest and stand still—do not budge an inch. Have somebody watch you with a stopwatch to time your progress, or else you will never believe this will work and so you will not even try the exercise, and your shoulder and the dog's neck will be traumatized for years to come.

Stand still and wait for the dog to stop pulling, and to sit and/or lie down. All dogs stop pulling and sit eventually. Most take only a couple of minutes; the all-time record is 22½ minutes. Time how long it takes. Gently praise the dog when she stops pulling, and as soon as she sits, enthusiastically praise the dog and take just one step forward, then immediately stand still. This single step usually demonstrates the ballistic reinforcing nature of pulling on leash; most dogs explode to the end of the leash, so be prepared for the strain. Stand firm and wait for the dog to sit again. Repeat this half a dozen times and you will probably notice a progressive reduction in the force of the dog's one-step explosions and a radical reduction in the time it takes for the dog to sit each time.

As the dog learns "Sit we go" and "Pull we stop," she will begin to walk forward calmly with each single step and automatically sit when you stop. Now try two steps before you stop. Wooooooo! Scary! When the dog has mastered two steps at a time, try for three. After each success, progressively increase the number of steps in the sequence: try four steps and then six, eight, ten and twenty steps before stopping. Congratulations! You are now walking the dog on leash.

Whenever walking with the dog (off leash or on leash), make sure you stop periodically to practice a few position commands and stays before instructing the dog to "Walk on!" (Remember, you want the dog to be compliant everywhere, not just in the kitchen when her dinner is at hand.) For example, stopping every 25 yards to briefly train the dog amounts to over 200 training interludes within a single 3-mile stroll. And each training session is in a different location. You will not believe the improvement within just the first mile of the first walk.

To put it another way, integrating training into a walk offers 200 separate opportunities to use the continuance of the walk as a reward to reinforce the dog's education. Moreover, some training interludes may comprise continuing education for the dog's walking skills: Alternate short periods of the dog walking calmly by your side with periods when the dog is allowed to sniff and investigate the environment. Now sniffing odors on the grass and meeting other dogs become rewards which reinforce the dog's calm and mannerly demeanor. Good Lord! Whatever next? Many enjoyable walks together of course. Happy trails!

CHAPTER NINE

Further Reading and Resources

BOOKS

About Golden Retrievers

Schlehr, Marcia. *The New Golden Retriever.* New York: Howell Book House, 1996.

About Health Care

American Kennel Club. *American Kennel Club Dog Care and Training.* New York: Howell Book House, 1991.

Carlson, Delbert, DVM, and James Giffen, MD. *Dog Owner's Home Veterinary Handbook.* New York: Howell Book House, 1992.

DeBitetto, James, DVM, and Sarah Hodgson. *You & Your Puppy.* New York: Howell Book House, 1995.

Schwartz, Stefanie, DVM. *First Aid for Dogs: An Owner's Guide to a Happy Healthy Pet.* New York: Howell Book House, 1998.

About Dog Shows

Hall, Lynn. *Dog Showing for Beginners.* New York: Howell Book House, 1994.

Vanacore, Connie. *Dog Showing, An Owner's Guide.* New York: Howell Book House, 1990.

About Training

Ammen, Amy. *Training in No Time.* New York: Howell Book House, 1995.

Dunbar, Ian, PhD, MRCVS. *Dr. Dunbar's Good Little Book.* James & Kenneth Publishers, 2140 Shattuck Ave. #2406, Berkeley, CA 94704. (510) 658-8588. Order from publisher.

Evans, Job Michael. *People, Pooches and Problems.* New York: Howell Book House, 1991.

About Activities

American Rescue Dog Association. *Search and Rescue Dogs.* New York: Howell Book House, 1991.

Daniels, Julie. *Enjoying Dog Agility—From Backyard to Competition.* New York: Doral Publishing, 1990.

O'Neil, Jackie. *All About Agility.* New York: Howell Book House, 1998.

Simmons-Moake, Jane. *Agility Training. The Fun Sport for All Dogs.* New York: Howell Book House, 1991.

Volhard, Jack and Wendy. *The Canine Good Citizen.* New York: Howell Book House, 1994.

MAGAZINES

The AKC GAZETTE, The Official Journal for the Sport of Purebred Dogs
American Kennel Club
51 Madison Ave.
New York, NY 10010

Dog Fancy
Fancy Publications
3 Burroughs
Irvine, CA 92718

Dog World
Maclean Hunter Publishing Corp.
29 N. Wacker Dr.
Chicago, IL 60606

Golden Retriever World
Hoflin Publishing, Inc.
4401 Zephyr St.
Wheat Ridge, CO 80033-3299

MORE INFORMATION ON GOLDEN RETRIEVERS

National Breed Club

GOLDEN RETRIEVER CLUB OF AMERICA
Ms. Catherine E. Bird, Secretary
2005 NE 78th St.
Kansas City, MO 64118

The club can give you information on all aspects of the breed, including the names and addresses of breed, obedience and hunting clubs in your area.

Resources

The American Kennel Club

The American Kennel Club, devoted to the advancement of purebred dogs, is the oldest and largest registry organization in this country. Every breed recognized by the AKC has a national (parent) club. National clubs are a great source of information on your breed. The affiliated clubs hold AKC events and use AKC rules to hold performance events, dog shows, educational programs, health clinics and training classes. The AKC staff is divided between offices in New York City and Raleigh, North Carolina. All registration functions are done in North Carolina.

For registration and performance events information, contact:

THE AMERICAN KENNEL CLUB
5580 Centerview Drive, Suite 200
Raleigh, NC 27606
Phone: (919) 233-9767
Fax: (919) 233-3627
E-mail: info@akc.org

For obedience information, contact:

THE AMERICAN KENNEL CLUB
51 Madison Ave.
New York, NY 10010
Phone: (212) 696-8276
Fax: (212) 696-8272
E-mail: www.akc.org

For information on AKC Companion Animal Recovery, contact:

Phone: (800) 252-7894
Fax: (919) 233-1290
E-mail: found@akc.org

INDEX